Beyond the Safety Net:

REVIVING THE PROMISE OF OPPORTUNITY IN AMERICA

By

Sar A. Levitan and Clifford M. Johnson

Ballinger Publishing Company
Cambridge, Massachusetts
A Subsidiary of Harper & Row, Publishers, Inc.

International Standard Book Number: 0-88730-013-8

Library of Congress Catalog Card Number: 84-9338

Printed in the United States of America

Library of Congress Cataloging in Publication Data

Levitan, Sar A.
  Beyond the safety net.

  Includes bibliographical references and index.
  1. United States—Social policy. 2. Public welfare—
United States—History. I. Johnson, Clifford M.
II. Title.
HV95.L53   1984   361.6'1'0973   84-9338
  ISBN 0-88730-013-8

Contents

Preface

The central thesis of *Beyond the Safety Net* is that the evolving welfare system is an appropriate and generally effective response to problems of unequal opportunity and poverty in modern America. We conclude that the welfare system has contributed broadly to the well being of Americans, but that it has failed to spur the expansion of employment opportunities at a pace consistent with gains in income security.

In this volume we attempt to trace the logic and rationale of conservatives in their approach to federal social welfare policy, considering separate and sometimes contradictory arguments on their individual merits. We find that the conservative view of America's social problems is sharply at odds with available evidence, and we endeavor to develop an alternative which more accurately reflects the nation's experience and fundamental values. We believe that the nation will extend fair and equal opportunities to all its citizens only when it returns to the notion of government responsibility in a modern welfare system.

When appropriate, we attempt to distinguish between the beliefs of New Right ideologues and those of mainstream conservatives. "Old" conservatives of the New Deal and postwar eras largely accept a federal role in mitigating the extreme hardships of free markets. In contrast, ascendant radicals of the political Right adhere to rigid notions of personal responsibility and initiative, thereby challenging even the most basic federal social welfare institutions. These distinctions, while not always sharp, are unavoidable in an accurate portrayal of modern conservative thought.

The considerable attention we devote to New Right ideology reflects its importance in federal social welfare policies since the 1980 elections. We draw liberally from policy statements of President Reagan and his administration officials in describing dominant right-wing views. In addition, we turn to laissez faire advocates, particularly George Gilder and Milton Friedman, who are recognized spokesmen for radical and mainstream conservative schools respectively. With Reagan the "prince" and Gilder and Friedman the preeminent "scribes" in the much-heralded resurgence of conservative ideology, we find a representative sampling of conservative opposition to the modern welfare system.

Conservatives come in all forms and sizes. Some conservatives recognize the inadequacy of laissez faire approaches to opportunity and social justice in modern America. By abandoning objections to federal social welfare interventions, they come closer to accepting the greater and more compassionate society which we envision. We welcome them to the fold.

Due in large part to conservative rhetoric, many Americans associate the welfare system with narrow income transfer programs for the poor rather than with its broader efforts to promote opportunity and equity for all income groups. A more factual analysis demonstrates that federal interventions have sharply reduced deprivation, broadened employment opportunities, improved prospects for self-sufficiency, and diminished fears of illness and old age.

The failings and disappointments of the welfare system are not ignored in this volume, but rather acknowledged as a natural outgrowth of ambitious attempts to solve complex social problems. Based on the experience during the past fifty years, the final chapter stresses the need for expanded aid to the working poor, greater flexibility in combining work and welfare, and more adequate employment and training opportunities. Recognizing the political obstacles to the further development of the welfare system, and the need to rein in some aspects of entitlement programs, we conclude that a majority coalition can be reconstructed when positive political leadership begins to restore public faith and confidence in government.

In preparing the final drafts of this manuscript, we are deeply indebted to Peter Carlson for his contributions in revising and adding to the documentation presented in the volume. We are grateful to Gordon Berlin, Prue Brown, Frank Gallo, and Robert Taggart for thoughtful criticisms and suggestions, Nadine Horenstein for encouragement, and Barbara Webster for putting the final touches to the manuscript.

Beyond the Safety Net was prepared under a grant from the Ford Foundation to The George Washington University's Center for Social Policy Studies. In accordance with the Foundation's practice, responsibility for the content was left completely to the authors.

Sar A. Levitan
Clifford M. Johnson

1

An Unfinished Agenda

We go through seasons of action, passion,
idealism, reform, and affirmative government
until our energies languish. Then we long for
respite and enter into seasons of doldrums,
drift, hedonism, cynicism, and negative
government.[1]

—Arthur Schlesinger, Jr.

The early 1980s have been a time of retrenchment in U.S. social welfare policy. As a nation we have scrutinized past commitments and curtailed existing programs. We have questioned the effectiveness of federal intervention and doubted our ability to expand opportunity or promote social justice. Perhaps this response was unavoidable, a necessary step in assimilating changes and reining in excesses from a prior era and defining our priorities for further progress. In this uncertain climate further retreat or the potential for social advancement rests heavily upon the turn of political events.

This period of retrenchment, like all others, has inflicted its costs. In the absence of a public consensus to move forward, aspirations for a more just and equitable society have been deferred. Poverty and unemployment rates have soared, reflecting lost opportunities to enhance self-sufficiency and provide productive work for the disadvantaged. The needs of the next generation have been largely ignored amid cynicism and resignation. When the nation's energy is rekindled and its sense of purpose restored, we will strive to regain the faith

1

and confidence that provide the foundation for a greater society.

The nation stands at a crossroads in 1984. President Reagan, labelling federal social welfare programs ineffective and destructive of cherished traditional values, has sought to dismantle major portions of the American welfare system. The administration's remaining liberal opponents were slow to counter this conservative assault in the wake of the 1980 Reagan election but have since marshaled their forces in strong defense of federal responsibilities for expanded opportunity and social justice. Not since the inauguration of Franklin Roosevelt's New Deal half a century ago have political views regarding government's role in promoting social welfare been so polarized.

A review of the evolution of the American welfare system demonstrates why the current confrontation may be pivotal, departing significantly from the terms of mainstream social policy debates in recent decades. In the postwar era conservatives and liberals came to share a basic belief in government's responsibility to protect Americans from extreme hardship and misfortune and to expand opportunities for them. The cornerstones of the welfare system—social security, Medicare, unemployment insurance, college grants and loans—grew so popular that they emerged as politically sacrosanct. Social policy battles between conservatives and liberals were joined less over the appropriate roles of government than over the necessary strategies and available means for alleviating social problems. Indeed, the greatest extensions of the modern welfare system were enacted under the conservative presidency of Richard Nixon with bipartisan congressional support, dwarfing in size and scope the initiatives of Lyndon Johnson's Great Society.

Since the election of Ronald Reagan, conservative opposition to established social welfare policies has become more stridently ideological and often radical in nature. To be sure, political realities have forced President Reagan to abandon some of his most fundamental assaults on the welfare state, including his frequently stated support for voluntary rather than compulsory participation in social security. However, his administration has repeatedly challenged other federal efforts to broaden opportunity and ensure equity for all Americans, arguing that they represent inappropriate and illegitimate roles for the federal government. By assailing federal social policies on both ideological and tactical grounds, Reagan has called into question the predominant philosophy of activist government which guided the development of the modern welfare system since the Great Depression. When the Reagan call for retrenchment is placed in historical perspective, the stark choice that he presents to the American people becomes evident.

THE EVOLVING WELFARE SYSTEM

The evolution of the American welfare system can be viewed as the product of both increasing public sensitivity to the defects of free markets and expanding resources for ameliorating social ills. As the nation grew more affluent the disparities in income and opportunity generated by laissez faire policies became more visible and the hardships imposed by free markets less tolerable. Conservatives by definition resisted the development of the emerging welfare system, seeking to minimize the instability or redistribution of wealth associated with federal social welfare interventions. Yet from the 1930s through the 1970s federal roles and responsibilities increased because liberals supported and conservatives conceded the public's desire to compensate for the inadequacies of free markets.

Prior to the 1930s the market's shortfalls in providing essential public goods such as national defense, universal education, or commercial development was the only broadly accepted rationale for a federal role in economic management and social welfare. In the United States expenditures for public goods preceded by more than a century other federal interventions to promote social welfare. Investments in canals, ports, and similar infrastructure proliferated in the early decades of the republic. The westward expansion was considered a legitimate public activity and proceeded under federal auspices. Even Thomas Jefferson, a consistent and eloquent opponent of federal expansion, invested public funds for the Louisiana Purchase which has turned out to be a profitable investment in real estate. The Morrill Act of 1862 created an extensive system of land grant colleges which subsequently revolutionized American agriculture, vividly demonstrating the importance of a federal role in the provision of public goods. Rural electrification and the development of the Tennessee Valley Authority are more recent examples of government investments that proved critical to the nation's social and economic development.

The deep and pervasive deprivation wrought by the Great Depression provided the catalyst for the extension of federal roles in economic management and social welfare. Limited insurance against destitution no doubt would have developed even in the absence of such dire and compelling economic conditions. In Europe basic government protections against the hardships of old age or infirmity predated the New Deal by many years, beginning with the rudimentary welfare states of Bismarck's Germany and Lloyd George's Britain. Throughout the civilized world growing affluence was accompanied by public outcries against the harshest of market outcomes and the gradual development of institutions to alleviate human suffering.

The evolution of the U.S. welfare system has mirrored this broader trend. Yet the turbulent experience of the 1930s clearly played a pivotal role in weaning the American public of its blind faith in free markets and heightening the legitimacy of government intervention.

The acceptance of Keynesian economic theories played an important role in the expansion of federal responsibilities. They dispelled the sense of impotence and resignation that had accompanied sharp economic downturns and destroyed the underlying fatalism that business cycles must run their course no matter what their toll in human suffering. Goals of economic management and humanitarian aid were highly compatible during the depression—public works projects and income transfers stimulated the economy while also offering help to those in need. Moreover, public recognition of a federal role in assisting the least fortunate remained strong even after the economy recovered and the majority of Americans prospered. To the extent that Keynes legitimized federal efforts to improve the functioning of free markets during economic downturns, it was a modest leap to extend the notion of government responsibility to those who failed to share in the affluence of the economy even during good times.

New Deal expansions of the federal role in social welfare focused initially on the most obvious victims of hard times: the unemployed, the aged, orphans, and the disabled. Beyond insurance against widespread joblessness the intent of early income support programs was to provide some measure of security for those who could not work or otherwise provide for themselves. The threat of poverty in the later years of life was pervasive in an era when few Americans earned retirement benefits and infirmity frequently prevented continuation of work activities. Work outside the home was also viewed, in light of the practices of the time, as inappropriate for widows with young children and rarely available for the blind and disabled. Since these groups constituted the traditional deserving poor, assistance to them naturally followed the acceptance of federal responsibility for the shortfalls of free markets.

The income transfer programs and collective bargaining statutes of the New Deal also represented an attempt to check the tendency of free markets to promote wide disparities in income and resources, allowing the "haves" to amass increasing wealth and the "have nots" to fall further into relative poverty. First by ensuring a basic income for the aged and disabled and subsequently by providing cash and in-kind assistance to the able-bodied poor, the federal government reduced the scope and severity of poverty during more than three decades following World War II. Expanded organizing and bargaining rights for unions also boosted the earnings of many workers, enabling them to share in the benefits of postwar prosperity and offering them greater job security and dignity in the workplace. These government interventions constituted explicit recognition that free markets could neither ensure a morally acceptable distribution of wealth in affluent industrial societies nor provide meaningful opportunities for advancement to those at the bottom of the income ladder. Although federal actions have not led to dramatic shifts in income distribution since World War II—the shares of national wealth controlled by the rich and poor have remained remarkably stable over the past three decades—government initiatives have prevented further skewing in favor of the well-to-do.

When economic growth resumed in the postwar period other failings of the market system became increasingly evident. Doors of economic opportunity opened to the great majority of Americans, and yet prospects for advancement among minorities and women remained bleak. Tradition barred women from occupational advances; blacks were afflicted by segregation in the South and less blatant discrimination in the North. Other segments of the population found their opportunities blocked by lack of education, limited job skills, or regional isolation. Gradually the evidence mounted that economic freedom and opportunity have meaning even during periods of sustained economic growth only if barriers to participation and advancement are removed through government action.

Expansion of federal social welfare roles during the past few decades has also been fueled by changes in society's concepts of deprivation and need. With rising affluence the nation's capacity for alleviating economic want increased and relative standards for assistance to the poor rose accordingly. A home without indoor plumbing, the norm in earlier generations, came to be considered substandard or unfit for habitation. The definition of basic necessities reached beyond food, shelter, and clothing to include energy in an era of rising fuel costs and perhaps, more recently, local telephone service in the wake of AT&T's divestiture. These shifts in government objectives were natural and appropriate adjustments to changing social and economic conditions. Conservatives and liberals both acknowledged that market mechanisms do not respond to the ascending goals that characterize an advanced and affluent civilized society.

By the late 1970s the shared desire of liberals and conservatives to reduce hardship and deprivation had fostered the development of a comprehensive and complex system of income transfers which came close to providing for the basic needs of all Americans. This reliance on income transfers aroused little conflict in an era of sustained economic growth, for it was supported by an expanding economic pie and left existing avenues and opportunities for individual advancement otherwise untouched. Yet, without the more difficult step of broadening access to economic opportunity, envisioned by anti-poverty architects as the essential counterpart to income security, mounting strains on the welfare system gradually eroded the political consensus regarding appropriate roles and responsibilities for the federal government. Mainstream political leaders, whether liberal or conservative, have not sought to dismantle the American welfare system, but they do offer competing explanations for the nation's social problems and diverging prescriptions for future action.

CONSERVATIVES: THE RUNAWAY WELFARE STATE

Although mainstream conservatives still accept the foundations of the modern welfare system, they have responded to the social turmoil and economic stagnation of the late 1970s with fears that the welfare state is out of control. The rapid expansion of major entitlement programs, particularly those indexed to inflation, left conservative lawmakers with little discretion in determining the size of federal social welfare expenditures or their rate of growth. Because conservative economic thought traditionally linked excessive federal spending and deficits with poor economic performance, conservatives perceived uncontrollable social welfare programs as a serious threat to future prosperity. Soaring inflation and interest rates in 1979 and 1980 simply confirmed for conservatives their belief that the welfare system must be streamlined and future growth contained.

The work disincentives implicit in a welfare system that relies heavily on income transfers to alleviate hardship and suffering has lent additional credence to the conservative thesis that federal social welfare expenditures undermine economic growth. With welfare stipends in several states equal to or even exceeding the returns of the lowest paying work, current income maintenance programs indeed threaten to erode work motivation and create a dependent underclass. Retaining images of the poor as morally deficient, however, conservatives are inclined to attribute welfare dependency to indolence or lack of discipline among recipients rather than to job deficits and other barriers to work and self-sufficiency facing low-income Americans. Modern conservative thought remains firmly rooted in dedication to free markets and faith in the potential for individual achievement. As a result conservatives view work disincentives as another indication that the welfare state has gone too far—a reminder that the extension of federal aid to individuals beyond those clearly incapable of self-support only rewards the unmotivated and penalizes the productive.

Perceived threats to economic stability and growth are not the sole impetus for recent conservative challenges to the welfare system. Along with concerns over economic deterioration, conservatives have reacted to federal interventions such as affirmative action programs which they interpret as assaults on individual achievement and merit. In government efforts to broaden access to economic opportunity and to compensate for prior deprivations, conservatives find an abandonment of their historical commitment to self-reliance and market rewards for individual talent and effort. Because they view the free market as the fairest gauge of individual merit and the common good, conservatives contend that special aid for those who fall behind in the economic race can only detract from equity and social justice.

Conservative opposition to the extension of opportunities for work and advancement is buttressed by underlying economic interests. The concern of conservatives for property rights and social stability renders them generally apprehensive of change, skeptical of human nature, and inclined to accept known shortcomings over an uncertain future. Although their economic motives are seldom made explicit, critics of the welfare system rely on free markets to promote the narrow self-interest of society's most advantaged members. Nostalgia for a social order glamorized in national folklore—an order that in reality never existed—broadens the appeal of conservative thought beyond the ranks of the affluent, but the effect of laissez faire policies nonetheless is to further the economic interests of the rich at the expense of the less fortunate.

By insisting that free markets provide adequate opportunities for the motivated and that federal efforts to broaden opportunity are inconsistent with market rewards based on merit, conservatives portray the future of the welfare system as hinging on a stark choice between economic growth and redistribution. Attempts to alleviate social ills through redistribution, they argue, will further undermine work incentives and restrict the nation's potential for economic growth. Furthermore, in the absence of sustained growth, conservatives stress the futility of income transfers that ·redistribute shares of a dwindling economic pie. The conservative prescription for trimming the modern welfare system is based on the belief that social problems will be more adequately redressed through economic growth rather than redistributive policies and the conviction that no alternative could obviate the need to choose between these two approaches.

The conservative critique of the American welfare system has raised important concerns. In crafting future social welfare policies, the nation cannot ignore the possibility that steps toward greater equity will dampen economic growth, that income transfers will destroy incentives to work and achieve, or that efforts to promote income security will spawn a permanent and dependent underclass. Conservatives have also offered reminders of the nation's meritocratic values, questioning the meaning of equal opportunity and thereby focusing the legitimate debate over concepts of fairness and social justice. With regard to the importance of these issues liberals and conservatives seldom differ. However, liberal analysis traces the problems of the modern welfare system to a different source, calling not for retrenchment but for a more balanced approach to the nation's social problems.

LIBERALS: NEGLECTED OPPORTUNITY

In accounting for the troubles of the modern welfare system, liberals praise the achievements of transfer payments but acknowledge the timidity of past efforts to broaden access to economic opportunity in America. They admit that the record of federal social welfare interventions is hardly unblemished but insist that federal programs have yielded substantial progress toward the alleviation of poverty and deprivation. Liberals suggest that the apparent shortcomings of the nation's welfare system stem from a failure to pursue the goal of expanded economic opportunity with the same vigor and commitment devoted to the goal of income security. The liberal interpretation rejects reductions in federal social welfare responsibility as counterproductive, arguing instead for the restoration of proper balance between income support and self-sufficiency through improved prospects for work for all Americans.

Liberals part company with conservative critics of the welfare system at an early stage, challenging the alleged link between growth in social welfare expenditures and poor economic performance over the past two decades. As an alternative explanation liberals cite the external strains of the Vietnam war and OPEC price hikes, the damages of which were magnified by misguided macroeconomic policies. In their view poor management of monetary and fiscal policies at key junctures can be more plausibly held responsible for the economic stagnation of the 1970s than the relatively modest and gradual expansion of the welfare system. Liberals find no grounds for claims that federal social welfare efforts are incompatible with sustained economic growth and contend that federal interventions may actually contribute to prosperity by enhancing the productivity of society's most disadvantaged members.

In response to the popular wisdom that federal social welfare programs have failed, liberals maintain that the efficacy of federal interventions has been obscured by unrealistic expectations and misinformation regarding program accomplishments. Given President Johnson's fanfare and visionary rhetoric, fledgling Great Society programs could never have matched promise with performance. The results of successful federal interventions often were not visible until years after programs were launched, generating frustration and leaving controversial efforts vulnerable to attack. Indeed, the clash between inflated expectations and modest or delayed results evoked strident criticism from both ends of the political spectrum: conservatives charged that federal programs were ineffective and should be repealed; liberal critics held that their impact was too modest and their scope too narrow.

Liberals suggest that expectations of rapid change also contributed to a persistent bias in early research evaluations of federal social programs. Hostile and even objective observers compared new and experimental projects to well-established programs or to hypothetical alternatives, thereby stressing their shortcomings while underestimating their long-term potential. Despite frequent attempts to address multiple goals—reaching beyond service delivery to foster institutional change and social integration—most evaluations ignored secondary objectives and nonquantifiable benefits. Waste and inefficiency, usually concealed from public view in the private sector, were scrutinized and widely publicized without meaningful bases of comparison. The negative effects of federal intervention, rather than being assessed as unavoidable trade-offs to be balanced against the costs of inaction, were treated in isolation as proof of misguided action and counterproductive results.

As with all attempts to address complex social problems, past strategies for alleviating poverty and expanding opportunity created new dilemmas and challenges even as they brought progress in resolving old ones. Medicare and Medicaid broadened access to health care services. At the same time they contributed to inflationary pressures in the health care industry. Unemployment insurance provided some income security for millions forced into idleness and yet in some cases also delayed job search. The availability of in-kind benefits reduced poverty but also added to serious inequities and perverse incentives in the treatment of the working poor. Aid to families without working parents improved the lot of impoverished children, and yet greater income security accelerated a discouraging rise in female-headed households with low earnings capacity, particularly among blacks.

The distinction between conservative and liberal views is that, while conservatives see the emergence of these new challenges as evidence of the failure of federal intervention, liberals accept them as an inevitable outgrowth of the process of change. In an advanced society, liberals contend, attempts to transform basic institutions or redistribute income and opportunity necessarily generate turmoil and social costs. Furthermore, because standards of deprivation and income adequacy are relative, liberals argue that societal goals advance in conjunction with the nation's rising affluence, posing new objects for appropriate federal concern. As Lyndon Johnson described his vision, we are not seeking "a safe harbor, a resting place, a final objective, a finished work" but rather "a challenge constantly renewed." In this context liberals find in contemporary problems a reason for renewed commitment rather than a cause for retreat.

In contrast to conservative claims that the poor are unmotivated, liberals assert that self-sufficiency through work for many Americans is rendered unattainable by slack labor markets, barriers to entry into stable employment, and wage rates often too low to lift even full-time workers and their families above the poverty level. As a result the least advantaged have been offered subsistence without hope or the dignity of employment, with predictable consequences for work disincentives and dependency. Thoughtful liberals do not defend every aspect of the welfare system that existed in 1980, recognizing the need to rein in programs that are no longer affordable and the value of periodic pruning to eliminate programs that have proved ineffective or outlived their usefulness. Yet the purpose of this pruning process for liberals is not retrenchment but revitalization: freed from some of the constraints of past interventions, they hope to foster a new commitment to the expansion of economic opportunity in America.

A RADICAL ASSAULT ON GOVERNMENT

In conjunction with society's periodic need to digest and sort through past initiatives, public fears of economic turmoil and decline may have rendered the retrenchment of recent years inevitable. The failure of successive administrations to relieve inflationary pressures, and the sense of economic insecurity spawned by rampant inflation, certainly restricted the potential for significant gains in social welfare and prescribed limits for future progress. While not justifying sharp reductions in federal social programs, energy shortages and rising international competition also heightened the nation's sense of vulnerability. Within these limits, however, a strong leader who resisted the temptation to blame the welfare state for national economic ills could have greatly enhanced the perceived legitimacy of federal intervention. In the absence of positive and forceful leadership to defend the social welfare efforts of the federal government, public confidence in the modern welfare system has been seriously undermined.

Under the Reagan administration, antigovernment ideology has emerged as the basis for a radical brand of conservatism that would dramatically restrict federal social welfare efforts. Capitalizing on feelings of alienation and powerlessness in modern America, right-wing ideologues have discovered that the federal government is a convenient scapegoat for complex problems. Campaigning against Washington offers obvious political advantages: it taps voter anxieties concerning national problems, provides simplistic explanations blaming a remote "enemy," and absolves conservatives of responsibility for the unpopular federal policies. Antigovernment rhetoric also appeals to underlying class interests, ratifying prejudices against the welfare system and justifying the greed that perpetuates the status quo. Although careful not to threaten entitlement programs and diverse tax expenditures that benefit the middle class and the affluent, incumbents as well as challengers have increasingly discovered the political virtues of attacking the federal establishment.

The forcefulness of President Reagan's radical rhetoric has caused some liberals to doubt the efficacy of federal intervention. The search of "neoliberals" for new approaches to social problems, when undertaken with confidence in the legitimacy and effectiveness of collective action through government, can be constructive and illuminating. Part of the challenge facing modern liberalism lies in the very difficulty of maintaining this openness to improvement and growth amid pressure from established constituencies in the welfare state. Yet today's neoliberals run the risk of going beyond critical self-examination to embrace the debilitating negativism of laissez faire ideology. As long as liberals are unwilling to defend the achievements of federal social welfare interventions, radical conservatives who perceive sharply limited roles for government will continue to dominate the course of public policy.

The strident antigovernment ideology of radical conservatives is based on a bleak view of human nature and the potential for government remedies. Drawing upon pathological views of poverty, which have their origin in Calvinist doctrine and Elizabethan laws, right-wing ideologues believe that the plight of the able-bodied poor stems from individual moral defects—most notably, indolence. Beyond providing a bare subsistence income for the "deserving poor" who are clearly incapable of self-support, radical conservatism endorses harsh treatment for the impoverished, confident that under the threat of deprivation the poor will find work or create their own jobs. President Reagan and his fellow ideologues begin with the premise that many Americans who fall below the poverty line are poor for want of trying. This assumption leads inevitably to resignation and to the conclusions that federal interventions offer more hindrance than help and that very little can be done to improve the lot of the less fortunate.

The demography of the poor sharply contradicts the ideological claim that poverty is primarily a moral problem. Nearly half of the adult non-aged poor work either part time or full time, and yet earn wages too low to lift their families out of poverty. Others are unable to enter the labor force because of mental or physical impediments or child care responsibilities. Most poor families neither remain below the poverty threshold for prolonged periods nor sustain a culture of poverty from generation to generation. Contrary to the mythology of the Right, the problems of low-income Americans stem from complex causes, including personal misfortunes and job deficits, and their efforts to meet basic needs through a combination of work and welfare bring only intermittent success.

Unlike their reasonable conservative counterparts, right-wing ideologues ignore both current conditions and social history in promoting their assault on government. As memories of prior eras have faded, radical conservatives have portrayed social programs as creating rather than eliminating barriers to economic advancement. As federal intervention has overshadowed state and local roles, they have imagined a usurpation of power rather than an unwillingness and inability among smaller jurisdictions to cope with pressing national needs. In attacking federal initiatives to address complex problems, they have misconstrued inevitable imperfections as evidence of their own futility. Consistently, conservative ideologues sacrifice a clear and balanced appraisal of past efforts in order to further their vision of free enterprise and limited government.

Radical conservatives defend their antigovernment ideology by resorting to a rigid anti-intellectualism which places faith and common sense before objective analysis. Because the judgments of experts are seen as diminishing personal responsibility, and perhaps because empirical observations contradict so many of their assumptions in social welfare policy, right-wing ideologues frequently deride the findings of research. In the face of contrary evidence, they pronounce the experts wrong and their conclusions irrelevant to the nation's problems.

The rejection of research findings is particularly evident in President Reagan's political ideology. Early in his political career Reagan discounted the complexity of national problems by asserting that there were "simple answers" to many of them and stressing that "the people have the genius and courage to solve their own problems."[2] As president, Reagan has presented his antipathy toward intellectuals and his commitment to faith over knowledge in starker terms:

> The truth is that Americans must choose between two drastically different points of view. One puts its faith in the pipe dreamers and margin-scribblers in Washington; the other believes in the collective wisdom of the people and their commitment to the American dream.
>
> [One] believes the solutions to our nation's problems lie in the psychiatrist's notes or in the social worker's file or in the bureaucrat's budget. We believe in the workingman's toil, the businessman's enterprise, and the clergyman's counsel.[3]

These comments are striking not only in the sharpness of the dichotomies they pose but also in their total denial of the value of empirical evidence and analysis. Faith and values are not only material; they represent *all* that is important.

This view of analysis and faith reflects a curious blend of metaphysics and political philosophy. Presumably, a reliance on experts and government decisionmaking thwarts "the human creativity that is indispensable to overcoming our problems" and traps us in "a very rational calculus of our affairs."[4] According to George Gilder, policy experts are "always wrong" because they frame issues too narrowly and because they underestimate the human potential that arises from faith and spiritual belief. This interpretation of the source of knowledge is reinforced by populist ideology. Thus, as one critic of the "politics of envy" described the alternative to liberal analysis, "A politics of economic and moral vision trusts the intelligence and creativity of all its people, whether rich or poor, in the hope that all together will create goods and services never imagined, for the greater good not only of our own nation but of all mankind."[5] To predict or study human behavior allegedly is to limit it; faith, not judgment, alone can inspire achievement and unleash the human spirit.

A predisposition against analysis fits well with the conviction of radical conservatives that social ills stem from moral deficiencies. By their nature, critics argue, empirical studies grossly overemphasize social and economic determinants of human behavior while ignoring the moral consequences of competing policy options. Gilder summed up this case against analysis:

> The Neo-Conservative believes not chiefly in principles but in empirical techniques. He believes that through study and analysis of social questions, one can arrive at reasonable conclusions . . . . Conservatives did not need twenty years of social analysis and computer regressions to determine that the War on Poverty with its Welfare Rights campaign was a sure failure. The New Right did not need multimillion-dollar income-maintenance experiments to discover that hard work, family, stability, and faith in God are indispensable to upward mobility.[6]

At best, research findings are irrelevant. At worst, they are dangerously misleading. In either case radical conservatism often does not refute empirical analysis but instead denies its legitimacy in public policy debates.

There are limits to the usefulness of research. Although the social sciences provide a wealth of information regarding human behavior, they cannot capture the complexities of the human spirit in a single set of principles or equations. The successes and the dangers of federal intervention can be identified through program evaluations, but assessments of their relative importance necessarily rest more heavily on value judgments than empirical observation. Researchers seldom emphasize the elements of uncertainty in their work, focusing on narrow questions that fit neatly within the scope of the analysis and yield quantifiable results. The larger issues of social welfare policy are appropriately resolved in the political domain, ideally by combining an informed assessment of our capabilities with a continuing awareness of our dreams.

Empirical findings cannot prove conclusively that the views of radical conservatives are incorrect. Although any assessment of the welfare system rests heavily upon normative judgments, the argument of this book is that attacks on federal social programs are replete with erroneous conclusions flowing from doubtful assumptions, that antigovernment ideologues offer no alternative means of bolstering opportunity and advancement for the nation's disadvantaged and working poor, and that federal action can lead to a more just and equitable society, the fruits of which will be broadly shared. The opposition of President Reagan and other radical conservatives to federal social welfare interventions ultimately rests upon a value choice that rejects the notion of collective responsibility and holds that we are not our brother's keeper. For those who make a different value choice, who share Samuel Johnson's view that "a decent provision for the poor is the true test of civilization," society can accept responsibility for the plight of those less fortunate and seek to evoke the best in their nature. With renewed confidence in government and with the humility that should accompany incomplete understanding, federal interventions can move us closer to fulfilling the promise of opportunity in America.

AN IMMEDIATE AGENDA

When the nation discards today's prevailing negativism it will turn to the urgent task of broadening access to opportunity for all Americans. The most glaring deficiency of past and present social programs lies in the nation's failure to couple income transfers to meet basic needs with opportunities for work and self-advancement. Its destructive impact is visible in the deprivations of the working poor, the disappearance of significant work incentives for welfare recipients, the hopelessness of a growing underclass left increasingly outside the mainstream of American society, and the denial of equal opportunity to large sectors of the population. The difficulties associated with the expansion of opportunity are substantial, ranging from the technical and economic to the cultural and political. Yet, if the ideal of an equitable society is ever to be realized, there is no alternative. Because barriers to opportunity accumulate at an early age, federal interventions should begin with educational programs to ensure a firm foundation in the basic skills necessary for future self-sufficiency. Enhanced compensatory education in primary schools, remedial programs for both in-school and out-of-school youth at the secondary level, and youth employment programs structured to strengthen the basic competencies of disadvantaged teenagers are essential components of an effective federal strategy to broaden opportunity. Research and demonstration projects have indicated the potential for dramatic educational gains through a combination of periodic competency testing and individualized, self-paced remedial instruction for youth with basic skills deficiencies. Unless federal education initiatives compensate for the obstacles encountered by less fortunate children, their prospects as adults will be sharply limited.

The broader extension of economic opportunity in adult years relies heavily upon the development of a comprehensive employment and training system. Recognizing that persons who experience difficulties in competing for sustained employment in the labor market have diverse needs, federal intervention should begin with providing the resources for a thorough assessment of individual skills and problems that would help program administrators determine the appropriate form of assistance. For workers with saleable skills or education credentials, a program facilitating job search may be sufficient to secure placement. Others lacking the basic competencies required even for entry-level jobs are best served by an intensive program of remedial basic education, with an opportunity for the successful to pursue more specific occupational training when justified by labor market demands. Employment in the private sector, while the primary objective of federal initiatives, should be supplemented through public job creation efforts when necessary to provide work experience for new entrants into the work force or to compensate for job deficits in slack labor markets.

The benefits of a comprehensive employment and training system would be broadly shared. Provided that the rewards of work exceed the stipends of public assistance, carefully structured training and employment opportunities for welfare recipients would offer a constructive alternative to punitive work requirements and long-term dependency. Supplemented by advance notification for plant closings and mass layoffs, the sequence of evaluation and screening, job search assistance, training, and last-resort public employment is sorely needed by workers in declining industries or occupations. Coupled with vigorous enforcement of antidiscrimination statutes, this approach to expanded employment opportunity also would reduce barriers to advancement based on race, sex, religion, or national origin. The provision of economic opportunity regardless of income will be possible only when productive work can be secured for all these groups.

Recent shifts in federal social welfare policy have run directly counter to the broader distribution of opportunity and income. President Reagan has spurned intensive remediation or job creation for the deficiently educated and unskilled, content instead to rely upon market forces to meet the labor demands of employers. Pressured by strong bipartisan congressional opposition, the Reagan administration acquiesced to limited training services to the unemployed and disadvantaged but denied stipends to those enrolled in training programs. Similarly, President Reagan has diminished opportunity by discouraging work effort among welfare recipients, refusing to allow them to retain a significant portion of their earned income. The cumulative result of the Reagan administration's policies has been to give the poor little hope of escaping poverty and those eligible for public assistance little incentive to seek work—outcomes that are antithetical to the goals of the modern welfare state.

In order to combine work and welfare in constructive ways, federal policy should channel significant aid to the working poor and bolster work incentives for welfare recipi-

ents. A negative income tax would offer the most comprehensive and equitable approach to the supplementation of
earned incomes, but widespread opposition to a guaranteed
income appears certain to preclude this option in the near
future. A more immediate strategy should build on existing
programs and benefits, expanding the earned income tax
credit to boost the living standards of the working poor and
reducing marginal tax rates in means-tested entitlements
serving low-income Americans. As national resources allow,
other steps should be taken to strengthen the social welfare
safety net, including establishment of a federal minimum
welfare benefit, extension of health care coverage to the
working poor, and special assistance to women heading
single-parent families. All these measures require the abandonment of the Reagan administration's harsh assault on
federal programs to assist those living in poverty.

The first priority of a social welfare agenda for the 1980s
must be to put the nation's economic house in order. The
Reagan administration's misguided tax cuts have eroded the
federal tax base needed for support of social welfare efforts.
An unprecedented peacetime military buildup has also contributed to record annual budget deficits of nearly $200 billion,
threatening economic stability and growth well into the
foreseeable future. No progress toward expanded opportunity
can be achieved until the federal tax base is restored and a
more balanced set of budget priorities adopted.

Assuming the damages of retrenchment are redressed
when positive leadership returns to the White House and
Congress, troubling obstacles to progress will linger. The costs
of universal entitlements have soared in recent years, divert-
ing resources from means-tested programs. The modern
welfare system will remain affordable only if the difficult
political task of trimming federal aid to the non-needy is
addressed. While the Reagan administration has done little to
curtail the expanding entitlements of middle- and upper-
income groups, its rhetorical pledges to target aid more

carefully to those in need accurately reflect one of the central challenges of the modern welfare state. Necessary reforms in existing programs include taxing benefits for nonpoor households with other income and by curtailing tax expenditures, reducing preferential treatment of special interests, and regulating costs in the provision of in-kind assistance.

By permitting unrestrained growth in aid to the nonpoor, the American welfare system has not kept pace with troubling new social problems, particularly those associated with the increasing numbers of single-parent families among the poor. Roughly half of all poor families are now headed by women, and female-headed families with children are nearly five times more likely to be poor than other households. Although intergenerational dependency and lack of work effort do not typify the poverty population as a whole, this conservative stereotype is frighteningly accurate for many poor female-headed families trapped in the welfare system. The feminization of poverty deserves a prominent place on the nation's social welfare agenda, for it threatens to create a permanent, dependent underclass with no significant hope of economic advancement and self-sufficiency.

Political uncertainties also cloud prospects for progress on a new social welfare agenda. Since the 1930s low- and middle-income Americans have joined with other groups to form a majority coalition in support of an expanded welfare system. The political constituency for federal social welfare efforts in the 1980s may prove less predictable and more difficult to marshal for victory at the polls. Organized labor, the traditional core of the liberal coalition, has been battered by economic troubles and political defeats. The ability of its leaders to forge coalitions for social justice has dwindled as portions of its membership have grown increasingly conservative in their political views. The civil rights movement has lost much of its urgency and support, largely due to earlier hard-won social and political victories. The middle class, which owes its affluence in large part to the flourishing of the welfare state, frequently perceives social welfare initiatives as endangering past gains rather than generating future economic opportunity.

The task of reconstructing a majority coalition to preserve the current welfare system, let alone to expand it, will require difficult choices and compromises. While channeling benefits to those most in need, the public's reluctance to support targeted federal assistance cannot be ignored. In strengthening the institutions that serve low-income populations, the need for more effective representation of the poor must be balanced against the dangers of political backlash in other segments of the community. No new ideas can rescue the nation's leaders from such unpleasant tradeoffs and internal divisions.

Without question, meaningful and sensible reform of the modern welfare system will prove extremely difficult. In an era of special interest groups and political action committees, stalemate and paralysis in government loom all too likely. The Reagan administration shattered the ideological deadlock of the 1970s with its dramatic retreat from social responsibility, and in some cases its spending cuts served a useful purpose, trimming the fat from federal social welfare efforts. Too frequently, however, Reagan's budget cuts have been crude and indiscriminate, reducing federal spending without regard to need or merit. Now it is time to swing the pendulum back in the other direction, to resume our efforts to revive the promise of opportunity in America.

Skeptics suggest that the modern welfare system has become a victim of its own success, providing avenues for advancement that deplete its base of political support. Indeed, under political leadership that denigrates the federal government as a vehicle for improving the common welfare and maligns social programs as a threat to prosperity, prospects for marshaling a broad base of support for social welfare initiatives are bleak. Yet the potential for constructing a majority coalition remains. Through a clearer understanding of past experience in social welfare, the modern welfare system can be shown to offer not only income and opportunity but also a more open and equitable society for all Americans. In this time of retrenchment no challenge is more important than refreshing our memory and refocusing our vision for the years ahead.

NOTES

1. Arthur Schlesinger, Jr., "Is Liberalism Dead?", *New York Times Magazine*, March 30, 1980, p. 73.
2. Ronald Reagan, *The Creative Society* (New York: The Devin-Adair Co., 1968), p. 20.
3. Ronald Reagan, October 4, 1982.
4. George Gilder, "Family, Faith and Economic Progress," *National Review*, April 15, 1983, pp. 428–29.
5. Michael Novak, "The Moral Case for Reaganomics," *National Review*, May 29, 1981, p. 614.
6. George Gilder, "Why I Am Not a Neo-Conservative," *National Review*, March 5, 1982, p. 219.

2

For Want of Trying

*We will continue to fulfill the obligations that
spring from our national conscience. Those who
through no fault of their own must depend on
the rest of us, the poverty-stricken, the disabled,
the elderly, all those with true need, can rest
assured that the social safety net of programs
they depend on are exempt from any cuts.*[1]

—*Ronald Reagan*

Conservative ideology is based on a reassuring view of
society. Imagining a world characterized by order and
certainty, conservatives hold that virtue is rewarded and
moral responsibility clearly assigned. Wealth is a mark of
distinction, representing the reward of individual effort and
hard work. Poverty, in contrast, is the just consequence of
personal inadequacies—physical frailty, mental deficiencies,
and behavioral defects. While alms are appropriate to relieve
the suffering of the sick or disabled, the destitution of the
corrupt or weak in spirit is just retribution for their misdeeds.
This emphasis on individual responsibility gives conservatives a comforting and compelling rationale for withholding
government efforts to alleviate poverty or to redistribute the
fruits of personal success.

Traditional arguments against government social welfare
initiatives appeal to our yearnings for an orderly universe that
rewards individual effort and accomplishment. The great
majority of Americans who are not poor already equate their

earnings capacity with moral worth, believing that their material comfort is a befitting and just return for their labors. Broader notions that we can control or substantially influence our personal destinies also strike a responsive chord, embodying the optimism on which all motivation depends in a civilized society. Finally, simple distinctions between the deserving poor and the deviant allow a compassionate response to the essential needs of those who cannot care for themselves and yet reinforce the moral conviction that sloth and vice should reap their own punishment.

The attractiveness of these underlying premises has rendered poverty theories based on individual characteristics extremely durable. The Western idea of poverty as a product of personal failings had its origins in Calvinist doctrine. Since the seventeenth century English poor laws this view has spawned repeated attempts in public relief measures to categorize and discipline the poor.[2] In the United States welfare policies have long sought to discourage dependency by stigmatizing recipients and focusing the most meager assistance on those who cannot work.[3] The policies and rhetoric of the Reagan administration have lent renewed currency in the 1980s to interpretations of poverty as a product of individual pathology.

The old belief that poverty is caused by individual inadequacies has resurfaced as the conceptual foundation of federal welfare policies despite dramatic changes in the nature of work and the structure of modern labor markets over the past two centuries. Whatever merit the presumed link between individual motivation and poverty may have had in agrarian societies, industrialization and more recent shifts toward a service-based economy have obliterated a world in which the willingness to work ensures a subsistence income. Modern conservative thought has failed to recognize many of the complexities of work and poverty in modern America, clinging instead to a view of the poor that contrasts sharply with available labor market evidence. As long as conservative beliefs remain rooted in wishful thinking rather than social and economic realities, prescriptions for federal retrenchment in social welfare, including the course adopted by the current administration, will be unwarranted and ultimately counter-productive.

HELPING THE TRULY NEEDY

The traditional debate regarding government roles in social welfare has centered upon competing definitions of the "deserving poor," now termed the "truly needy." Conservative arguments rest upon a very narrow definition, emphasizing physical or mental barriers to employability while presuming that healthy adults are capable of self-support. Even the staunchest opponents of government intervention to alleviate poverty endorse public assistance to the aged, sick, disabled, and mentally retarded. Yet conservatives fail to extend their concept of the truly needy to include the plight of the able-bodied poor.

Implicit in calls for sharp curtailments of federal aid to the poor is a conviction among conservatives that they can differentiate between the deserving and the unworthy. Welfare critics such as former Reagan adviser Martin Anderson contend that these judgments can be straightforward and objective:

> If we assume that our welfare system is to provide help to the needy only, it then follows that either a person has a valid need for welfare payments and should be on the welfare rolls or that person does not have a valid need for welfare payments and should not be on the welfare rolls.... If a person is capable of taking care of himself, he is independent and should not qualify for any amount of welfare.[4]

Disparities between an individual's presumed capacity for self-support and actual labor market experience do not dissuade opponents of government intervention from defining the truly needy in narrow terms. In conservative ideology the failure of the undeserving poor to achieve self-sufficiency only demonstrates the lack of motivation from which their poverty stems.

Provision of public assistance to all those in need, without regard to the causes of poverty, is disturbing to laissez faire adherents because they believe such provisions create a moral hazard, tempting individuals to choose idleness and dependency as an alternative to work at low wages.[5] Conservatives contend that current welfare policies already pose this danger, providing benefits to individuals without real need. President Reagan periodically contends that federal bureaucrats have expanded social programs well beyond their legitimate purposes:

> Having taken care of the people that are really in need . . . they begin to raise the standards for eligibility so that people who don't have real need are getting benefits. All the cuts that we have made in such programs are aimed at taking people off those programs that really are not morally justified in being there.[6]

In a similar vein President Reagan has suggested that the federal bureaucracy actively perpetuates poverty, claiming that "the war on poverty created a great new upper-middle class of bureaucrats who found they had a fine career as long as they could keep enough needy people there to justify their existence."[7] The necessary response allegedly is a return to a more exacting standard for identification of the deserving poor—one that limits bureaucratic discretion and purges persons who might be able to work from the welfare rolls.

Variations on the theme of aid to the non-needy abound. Milton and Rose Friedman perceive waste and ineffectiveness as the inevitable result of bureaucrats "spending someone else's money," and they conclude that federal aid increases poverty by reasoning that "if you start paying people to be poor, you're going to have a lot of poor people."[8] President Reagan's 1984 budget message urging reductions in welfare spending repeatedly turned to themes of waste, fraud, and abuse, claiming that "there is a lot of it out there" and that "the truly needy suffer, as funds intended for them are taken by the greedy."[9] Presidential counselor Edwin Meese went so far as to contend that Americans lining up for meals at soup kitchens could afford to pay for their food but nonetheless go to charity centers "because the food is free and that's easier than paying for it."[10] The message is unmistakable: human weakness, dishonesty, and ineptitude raise federal social welfare expenditures far higher than what would be required to care for the truly needy or deserving poor.

The belief that government aid is channeled to those who do not deserve it leads to two fundamental policy prescriptions. First, in order to avoid rewards for the unmotivated, welfare eligibility should be sharply restricted. The poor need what George Gilder terms "the spur of their poverty," the reminder that "to escape poverty they will have to keep their families together at all costs and will have to work harder than the classes above them."[11] Presumably, the poor have insufficient reason to work unless their very survival is at stake, and they cannot be protected from the "stick of the market . . . without diminishing their motivation and sentencing them to perpetual dependency."[12] Social welfare programs are seen as exacerbating the problem of poverty by robbing the poor of the necessary incentives to improve their own condition through work, an option open to all but the truly needy.

Second, because social welfare programs reach well beyond the ranks of the truly needy and allow the able bodied to avoid work, a prime goal of welfare reform should be to reduce the number of recipients. While the minimization of dependency is an objective shared across the ideological spectrum, President Reagan has sought to achieve this end directly through contraction of the welfare system rather than through related efforts to expand employment opportunities or increase earned incomes. He identifies shrinkage of the welfare rolls as *the* criterion for judging the success of government aid to the poor:

> If welfare in this country were truly successful, each year we would be able to point to how many people we had been able to make self-sustaining and independent.... Now, naturally, we're not talking about the disabled or anything. We're talking about able-bodied people. But, instead, if you look back at the history of it, welfare has been increasing in numbers, even when times are good.[13]

This logic overlooks a host of obvious facts about income transfers: they attempt simply to meet basic needs, they offer no substitute for employment and training programs which bolster earnings capacity, and they expanded during successive Democratic and Republican administrations prior to Reagan because there were a lot of poor people in America who needed the help. Nonetheless, conservatives contend reduction of the welfare rolls is important because the indolent and undeserving poor are living on the dole, mocking social justice by making no effort to help themselves.

Hidden behind these conclusions about poverty and social justice are misguided premises concerning the American labor market and the welfare population. Some of these underlying assumptions are evident: the poor are unmotivated, jobs are available for those willing to work, and the receipt of public assistance generates dependency. Other premises are rarely explicit: welfare recipients remain dependent on public support from generation to generation, the labor market serves all comers without discrimination, and wage levels are adequate to lift workers out of poverty. These assumptions are defended by anecdote or offered as tenets of faith, ignoring a considerable body of evidence regarding the workings of the labor market and the characteristics of the poor. A more accurate appraisal of the nature of work and poverty exposes the numerous discrepancies between traditional views of limited government responsibility and realistic requirements for social justice in modern America.

MOTIVATION AMONG THE POOR

At the heart of conservative opposition to welfare initiatives lies the suspicion that the poor are morally different from the nonpoor—that they do not share the values and aspirations of working Americans, that they do not respond to the incentives and opportunities of the market in the same way as the more prosperous. Although a very old idea, the association of poverty with deviance seems to acquire new life in every generation. Conservatives seldom question whether deviant lifestyles are of the poor's own choosing or simply reflect the harsh realities of deprivation. They are content to believe that the poor are unmotivated and unwilling to work unless coerced to do so.

The presumption that the poor shirk work responsibilities is most explicit in workfare initiatives which require welfare recipients to work off the support they receive. As advocated by the Reagan administration, workfare is intended primarily to deter persons from applying for welfare benefits as a preferred alternative to work. Mandatory workfare programs serving Aid to Families with Dependent Children (AFDC) and food stamp recipients presumably would "help ensure that labor force attachments are retained or gained" and "encourage recipients to find work in the private sector or perform useful public services when no private job is available."[14] Those discouraged from applying for welfare benefits because of work requirements by definition do not fall within the category of the truly needy, for persons with desperate need for help—those who should be eligible for welfare in the first place—would not hesitate to apply under such conditions.[15]

Workfare programs could be both successful and beneficial if they offered the dignity or the experience of constructive employment to the 10–15 percent of the AFDC population which realistically may be capable of self-support. Given careful screening, pre-employment counseling and sufficient incentives, welfare recipients could go far toward developing positive work habits and escape poverty. The provision of meaningful jobs at their existing wage scale could induce welfare recipients to voluntarily opt for workfare, eliminating some of the more distasteful associations of the programs with punishment for perceived moral deviance. The programs could then be assessed on the basis of the numbers who secured permanent employment and the level of their earnings.

Conservatives, however, seem to measure the success of workfare programs in terms of reduced caseloads rather than job placements. Beginning from the premise that welfare recipients are shunning the burdens of work, they generally refuse to invest the federal resources necessary to incorporate adequate training and work supervision in workfare projects. Local governments which have implemented the Reagan administration workfare concept have faced increased costs and seldom found the wherewithal to develop effective projects. Not surprisingly, state and local enthusiasm for workfare has remained low—while 23 states have authorized workfare projects for AFDC recipients, only 679 of the nation's 3,105 counties operated programs in 1983 and a mere 13 counties extended participation to food stamp recipients.[16]

In the belief that a large segment of the poor lack motivation and the willingness to work, conservatives also criticize the use of financial incentives to encourage work effort among welfare recipients. According to their argument poor individuals have an interest in work if they have no other way to support themselves, but the existence of social programs provides a corrupting alternative. This "moral" problem of avoiding work, it is claimed, cannot be resolved by financial appeals to a recipient's self-interest.[17] Martin Anderson extended this line of argument by contending that work incentives are "faulty in principle" because they "attempt to *persuade* people to do something they should be *required to do*" (author's emphasis). Anderson proposes that those "capable of self-support" be given reasonable notice and then removed from the welfare rolls.[18]

No doubt it is important to induce welfare recipients to seek work, so that necessity and rational self-interest do not render long-term dependency an unavoidable choice. Yet traditional concerns for the vitality of the work ethic among the poor merit far less attention than they receive in contemporary American society. Notwithstanding moralistic assaults on the character of the poor, the causes of poverty today are varied and complex. Most of those on welfare suffer from old age, disability, ill health, family disruption, unemployment, underemployment, low wages, poor training, or some combination of these conditions.[19] Barring some anecdotes a considerable body of evidence suggests that the work motivation of the poor is at least equal to that of the nonpoor in the United States. The presumption that the poor are unwilling to work and must be compelled to support themselves certainly has no adequate empirical basis.

MOVEMENT OUT OF POVERTY

Essential to the claim that poverty stems from a lack of work motivation is an image of the poor as a stagnant population living in perpetual dependency. If the poor are morally different from the rest of society, unwilling to exert themselves for their own support or advancement, they can be expected to remain forever in the lowest income ranks with little fluctuation or upward mobility. Conversely, if the composition of the poor changes rapidly, with some achieving self-sufficiency while others lose their capacity for self-support, the link between poverty and moral character is more difficult to discern.

The premise of a static poverty population is made explicit in prophecies of permanent welfare dependency. Milton and Rose Friedman have asserted that "the country is increasingly divided into two classes of citizens, one receiving relief and the other paying for it."[20] Martin Anderson has expanded on this notion, stating that the welfare system has "created a new caste of Americans . . . free from basic wants but almost totally dependent on the State, with little hope or prospects of breaking free."[21] By giving benefits to the poor "while expecting nothing in return" social programs allegedly "govern the lives of much of the underclass" and "undercut the mores about public behavior that the disadvantaged would have to assume to enter more fully into American life."[22] Common to these descriptions of the welfare poor is the belief in sharp and lasting distinctions between the poor and the rest of society, including a border between the lands of dependency and self-sufficiency that is seldom crossed, or at least rarely in the right direction.

For a small segment of the poor, movement out of poverty is limited and the dangers of long-term dependency are real. Basing his conclusion on a detailed study of persons in this category, Ken Auletta stated that the "underclass" poor suffer serious behavioral problems that are not representative of the poverty population as a whole:

> This group operates outside of organized society as we know it. Some are hostile to society, others afraid of it. As a group, they lack job and social skills, work habits, education, self-confidence; many are hostile, sometimes toward society, sometimes toward themselves. In this sense their problem is behavioral . . . . Antipoverty efforts that just throw money at this group of Americans are destined to fail.[23]

Particularly because the long-term afflictions of the underclass may be a product of misguided past practices, federal policy cannot ignore its special needs. However, the numerous problems of the underclass do not justify the indiscriminate slander of impoverished Americans' motivation and moral character on which criticisms of social programs often rest.

Contrary to popular wisdom the poverty population is far from static. Households frequently move in and out of poverty as circumstances of the poor respond to economic conditions and fluctuate with demographic changes. Longitudinal studies conducted at the University of Michigan have found that the children in four out of five families will escape their parents' poverty. In addition, over nearly a decade the surveys revealed that less than 2 percent of the sample lived in poverty throughout, even though one-fourth of the total were poor at some time during that period.[24] Rather than being a stagnant mass of individuals who are perpetually impoverished, the poor are largely persons who suffer deprivation of varying duration depending in large part on what Henry Aaron terms "random events"—business conditions, personal difficulties, structural changes in the economy, and a host of other factors that can alter a family's capacity for self-support.[25]

A survey of the poor also shows that an intermingling of work and welfare is far more common than a lifetime of dependency. For example, in 1979 (the most recent year in which such data were compiled) nearly three of every ten AFDC families had received welfare benefits for less than one year, and a majority of families had remained on the rolls for less than four years. Fewer than 8 percent of all AFDC families had received assistance without interruption for more than ten years, thereby approaching a generation of long-term dependency.[26] Research tracking the welfare participation of a representative sample of 5,000 families throughout the 1970s has yielded similar findings: while the percentage of the total population receiving public assistance in a given year remained a constant 10 percent between 1969 and 1978, fully one-quarter of the population received benefits in at least one of those ten years. Only 2 percent were dependent on welfare for their primary support for more than eight years of the survey period.[27]

The structure of federal welfare programs reflects the predominance of intermittent or part-time work among the poor. Unemployment insurance, a major component of the income maintenance system, is designed explicitly to cushion the impact of employment fluctuations in seasonal or highly cyclical sectors of the economy, effectively subsidizing wages in those industries. Federal welfare programs also provide some flexibility for sustained work effort among employable welfare recipients: within AFDC families more than half of the mothers available for work were employed or seeking jobs in 1979; 85 percent of employable fathers were also in the labor force.[28] This kaleidoscopic mixture of work and welfare among low-income groups belies claims that the poor are morally different from the rest of society and calls into question other premises on which traditional laissez faire arguments rest: that jobs offering steady employment are available to the motivated, that work offers escape from poverty and depriva- tion, and that the receipt of government assistance leads to permanent dependency.

THE AVAILABILITY OF JOBS

Conservatives have succeeded in challenging the willing- ness of the poor to work largely by treating job availability as a given. Recognizing that poverty and work motivation can be plausibly linked only if jobs are available for those who seek them, they profess confidence in market mechanisms while ignoring the evident lack of employment opportunities for millions of Americans, not only in recessions but also in good times.

The most vivid examples of refusal to acknowledge labor market conditions can be found in President Reagan's faith in job availability amid postwar record unemployment. During the worst recession since the Great Depression, Reagan clung to the theme that opportunities for work abound:

> Pick up the Sunday paper and look at the number of help wanted ads. Here are employers begging for employees, taking ads out for them at a time of the highest unemployment that we've known since the war.[29]

> In the great metropolitan centers ... you count as many as 65 pages of help wanted ads .... These newspaper ads convinced us that there are jobs waiting and people not trained for those jobs.[30]

The administration's only concession to widespread joblessness lay in the acknowledgment that workers with a record of
sustained employment may lack the skills to obtain available
jobs.

Except when unemployment reaches well into the middle
class, the mismatch between available work opportunities and
the skills of the unemployed receives scant attention from
conservatives. Lack of skills may explain joblessness among
the nonneedy, but it is assumed that the poor are suited only
for unskilled work and unwilling to work at commensurate
wages. The presumption of job availability remains:

> There are unskilled and low-skilled job openings around galore—
> but why should welfare recipients take them? Poor people may
> often be of low intelligence, but they are not stupid. Why should
> they work? Hundreds of thousands of low-skilled jobs are going
> begging in state employment offices. Metropolitan newspapers
> carry many pages of "help wanted" advertising.[31]

The availability of unskilled employment is rarely substanti-
ated, and yet this premise is crucial to the finding that "there
are millions of persons who will settle for small but easily
obtainable income if it enables them to avoid work."[32]

Perhaps the ultimate defense of the motivation thesis has
been crafted by George Gilder, who contends that individuals
can "create their own jobs" because "their supplies of work
and human capital can engender their own demand."[33]
Gilder's vision is one in which every person, however bereft
of resources, is an entrepreneur who can reap economic gains
simply through perseverence and hard work. A similar belief
in individual empowerment has led another conservative
observer to label poverty and unemployment in New York
City a "state of mind," concluding that "in a metropolis those
willing to accept any work—not holding out for something
meaningful and ennobling—can make a living and even save
money."[34] Opponents of government intervention believe, as
a tenet of faith, in the supremacy of motivation and will. By
definition, the problem of job availability no longer exists.

The conservative view of job availability, however comforting, is sharply at odds with labor market data. Job deficits in the private labor market fluctuate with business cycles, swelling dramatically during recessions—for example, the unemployment rate jumped from 5.7 percent in mid-1979 to 10.8 percent in December 1982. At the peak of this most recent recession a total of 12 million Americans were out of work, another 6.6 million were forced to settle for part-time employment, and 1.8 million abandoned the search for work because of the discouraging prospects in a slack labor market. The fact that so many individuals in all income groups continued to look for jobs amid deteriorating employment conditions is itself a testament to the strength of the work ethic in modern America.

Anecdotal evidence gleaned from the help wanted page does not refute the persistence of job deficits. Investigations of President Reagan's claims of job openings have revealed that employment advertisements are dominated by highly specialized occupations and frequently placed to fulfill the requirements of equal opportunity hiring procedures. For example, an American Vocational Association survey of vacancy listings placed in *The Washington Post*, found that 92 percent of publicized jobs required some training, and nearly three-fourths announced highly skilled positions. Others have documented that the volume of help wanted advertisements during the recent recession fell far below normal levels. Although manpower shortages persist in skilled and highly technical occupations, the presumption that entry-level jobs are widely available in slack labor markets is simply not credible.

Along with deficient aggregate demand, a variety of other factors can restrict individual employment prospects. Labor surplus areas persist in older industrial cities or in remote rural areas even during periods of relatively high employment nationally. Structural changes in the economy, whether fueled by technological change or foreign competition, also skew the geographic distribution of employment opportunities. Finally, racial discrimination, lack of skills, and diverse individual handicaps can render job openings meaningless for persons at the end of the job queue, leaving no practical option for gainful employment and self-sufficiency.

Job deficits for selected groups have persisted despite strong growth in the national economy. During the relatively prosperous 1950s, reductions in demand for U.S. coal, textiles, and other domestically manufactured consumer products created depressed areas in the Northeast and Appalachian regions. Despite the manpower requirements of the Vietnam war, inner city areas continued to suffer serious job shortages in the high employment years of the late 1960s. Unemployment rates crept upward with each successive recession during the 1970s, never returning to their prior levels. Throughout these trials the work attachment of disadvantaged groups has remained strong, and widespread joblessness has triggered no mass exodus from the labor force.

The data provide ample basis for viewing with great skepticism the implicit claim of opponents of social programs that the major obstacles to employment and self-support among the poor are lack of motivation and unwillingness to work. Further, the composition of the poor population indicates that greater job availability itself would not resolve the poverty problem. A large number of Americans live in poverty in spite of their ability to find and retain full-time employment. To the extent that conservatives trace the causes of poverty to the moral character of the poor, they mock the struggles of millions who work for a living but fail to earn an income adequate to reach even the poverty threshold.

WORKING TO ESCAPE POVERTY

A nation committed to social justice has an obvious interest in productive work as an alternative to welfare dependency. Gainful employment lessens the drain of income maintenance on limited public resources and provides the individual with a sense of dignity and hope. It is hardly surprising that the goal of moving welfare recipients off the rolls and into private employment is embraced across political and ideological spectra.

The emphasis on work as an alternative to welfare becomes more problematic when work is touted as offering certain escape from poverty. Opponents of government intervention contend that modern American society provides ample opportunities for upward mobility, allowing the motivated and industrious among the poor to lift themselves out of poverty through hard work. This portrayal depicts a labor market in which performance yields promotions, and achievement is a function of individual effort. An inevitable conclusion, given this perspective, is that those who languish in poverty do so as a result of their own shortcomings—their lack of motivation and commitment paramount among them.

The potential for self-advancement through work has been asserted most forcefully by George Gilder. Calling the United States "probably the most mobile society in the history of the world," he professes unbounded faith in progress through personal effort and stresses that escape from poverty "still inexorably depends on work."[35] In his view every successful ethnic group in American history escaped from poverty by working harder than other classes—a struggle in low-paying jobs which today's poor presumably are unwilling to undertake.[36] The culmination of Gilder's argument can be found in his conviction that the rich and poor are unable to live in close proximity without tension because "all but the supremely rich know they can plummet down, and the poor know that their condition is to a great degree their own fault or choice."[37]

President Reagan demonstrates a similar allegiance to the Horatio Alger dream of unlimited opportunities for self-advancement. The potential for upward mobility defines his sense of America: "What I want to see above all else is that this country remains a country where someone can always get rich. That's the thing that we have and that must be preserved."[38] Reagan's outlook transcends hopes for a prosperous society. Extrapolating from his own modest beginnings, Reagan appears to believe that every American has the chance to rise from rags to riches and that those who suffer bleaker fortunes have only themselves to blame.

While the goal of an open and affluent society is broadly accepted, it is grossly misleading to suggest that upward mobility through work in itself offers a meaningful solution to the problems of welfare recipients. Seventy percent of all AFDC recipients are children, most of whom are below working age. Of the remaining 30 percent a majority are precluded from working by mental handicaps, physical disabilities, or childrearing responsibilities. The most ambitious demonstration projects undertaken to encourage work among welfare recipients have been applicable to a mere 15 percent of the AFDC population. Opponents of social welfare programs perpetuate the myth that work is a realistic option for most welfare recipients, that only the spirit is weak. Yet innumerable studies have shown that social, economic, and personal circumstances are far better predictors of welfare dependency than is any aversion to the work ethic.[39]

Even for recipients deemed employable, the private labor market is seldom capable of providing an adequate income. One in four AFDC mothers has no work experience, and those with a record of prior employment are heavily concentrated in low-paying occupations, including service and clerical workers, laborers, operatives, and private household workers.[40] Without skills and valuable work experience the employable minority on the welfare rolls rarely gain access to jobs with decent wages, long-term stability, and opportunities for advancement—the attributes of a *good job* which alone can provide an escape route from poverty.[41] The earnings capacity of most welfare recipients certainly does not exceed that of the working poor, an indication that even steady employment for the welfare poor would not ensure their self-sufficiency.

The plight of the working poor contradicts most starkly the claim that an ardent commitment to work can ensure a life free of deprivation. In 1982 more than 9 million Americans worked during some part of the year and yet lived in poverty. Almost a third of these poor workers—nearly 3 million—labored the entire year but were paid wages too meager to offer them escape from indigence.[42] The image of the lazy and unmotivated choosing poverty in order to avoid work is irrelevant to this large body of impoverished Americans, whose devotion to the work ethic is tested to a far greater degree than that of more affluent workers.

In response to the grim realities of the working poor, conservatives reiterate their faith in upward mobility for the industrious and talented. If their optimism regarding prospects for advancement were warranted, the problems of the working poor could be accepted as either a temporary affliction or the fate of those lacking motivation and talent. Unfortunately, there is little reason to believe that mobility is a function of individual effort in modern America. The persistence of secondary labor markets, barriers to entry in selected occupations, and discriminatory employment practices all limit opportunities for advancement and self-sufficiency through work.

Current labor market conditions strongly support the hypothesis that the labor market is segmented, offering relatively high wages, good working conditions, job security, and chances for advancement to the majority of American workers while providing the rest with low pay, poor working conditions, unstable jobs, and few promotion opportunities.[43] Because workers in secondary markets are often forced to accept intermittent employment, their incomes tend to fall short of their full-time earnings capacity and below the poverty line. Moreover, since the working poor frequently hold unskilled jobs, they are unlikely to acquire higher skills on their jobs that would assist them in the transition from secondary to primary labor markets. The existence of primary and secondary markets side by side leaves unskilled workers trapped in dead-end jobs in which their motivation and effort have no appreciable impact on future advancement or capacity for self-support.

Patterns of labor market segmentation are strengthened and influenced by racial discrimination and barriers to occupational entry that hinder the advancement of disadvantaged minorities. Some progress has been made, as a direct result of federal mandates and interventions, in reducing the prevalence of discriminatory employment practices. Nonetheless, with rising levels of educational attainment and aggregate unemployment, the use of credentials or licensing requirements as barriers to entry in the primary labor market probably has increased in recent years. Both factors continue to frustrate the efforts of the disadvantaged to pull themselves out of poverty.

In the face of these obstacles to upward mobility, the commitment to work among disadvantaged groups persists nevertheless. An analysis of data from the 1979 national longitudinal survey of youth labor market experience found that, holding constant human capital, family background, and environmental variables, black youth are more willing than their white counterparts to take jobs paying less than the minimum wage.[44] The evidence also indicates that minorities travel farther to their jobs, further reflecting the strength of their labor force attachment. When thousands of candidates assemble in urban areas to apply for a few entry-level jobs and the great majority of the working poor continue to work for marginal financial rewards, it seems clear that the predominant causes of poverty lie beyond a willingness to work. Blacks from lower quantile socioeconomic status are also more likely to go to college than whites sharing the same status.

Poor prospects for advancement and inability to earn wages sufficiently high to lift families above the poverty level have taken their greatest toll among older black men. As recently as 1960 the labor force participation rates of white men and black men were identical; since that time participation rates for black males have fallen from 83 to 71 percent while that of whites dropped more modestly to 77 percent. Some analysts have seized upon the declining participation and higher unemployment rates of black men as evidence that they refuse to accept jobs and prefer welfare to work. The observation is partially accurate: regardless of race, the advantages of holding a low-paying job with intermittent forced idleness in the secondary labor market, compared to a life of crime or welfare dependency, have diminished over the past two decades. Not surprisingly, a segment of American society finds criminal activities or unreported work in the underground economy an attractive alternative to dead-end employment at subsistence wages. However, the crux of the problem lies not in the willingness of black men and other segments of the disadvantaged to work but in the inadequacy of prevailing wage rates and earnings in the secondary labor market.

The fundamental conflict between the goal of alleviating poverty and the economic interests of employers who rely on a ready supply of low-wage labor has long stymied progress toward social justice. If the returns of low-paying work are not enhanced, employment for many unskilled, deficiently educated, and discriminated against workers will provide no escape from poverty. If subsidized employment is offered to ensure an adequate income for workers and their families, millions of low-wage workers in unsubsidized jobs will seek such employment. Policies that emphasize work effort among the poor while ignoring their limited earnings capacity may serve the needs of employers for low-wage labor but will not lift the working poor to self-sufficiency. Furthermore, as long as workers remain poor despite their labors there can be no hope of reconciling the demands of equity and compassion in the treatment of the nonworking poor.

The case for improving work in secondary labor markets, through changes in tax and incomes policies, has been summarized succinctly by Nathan Glazer:

> If one reason for welfare is the abandoning of families by men who cannot get steady jobs, or whose jobs simply do not provide enough for themselves and their family, an effort to improve poor

jobs will have an effect. If another reason for welfare is the unattractiveness to many mothers of the jobs they could get, this approach will also have an effect . . . . It requires no measure of compulsion to get people to work, and it adds to the attractiveness and, we might say, the dignity of work.[45]

The adoption of public policies to supplement the earnings of the working poor is thwarted primarily by concerns for "dependency" and traditional beliefs in work as the solution to poverty. Only when federal policy ceases to treat work and poverty as mutually exclusive will it be possible to construct a more rational approach to the problems of needy Americans.

THE MEANING OF DEPENDENCY

Opponents of federal welfare policies tend to equate the receipt of public assistance with dependency: if an individual draws funds from the public coffers, that person is dependent. This notion of dependency makes no significant distinction between those who rely on welfare as their sole source of support, those who secure assistance to supplement their meager earnings, and those who receive stipends or grants while undergoing training or attending school. Success in battling dependency presumably can be measured by changes in the size of the welfare rolls. Hence, efforts to reduce poverty through income transfers by definition exacerbate the problem of welfare dependency.

The distillation of many degrees of reliance on welfare assistance into the extremes of total dependency and self-sufficiency has become a hallmark of Reagan administration welfare policies. Beyond provisions for those who cannot work (the deserving poor) the administration contends that federal benefits should be limited to temporary relief for those who should support themselves. President Reagan has argued that federal social programs frequently "destroyed pride and created a feeling of helplessness among those who needed encouragement and hope."[46] According to David Stockman, the Reagan administration's director of the Office of Management and Budget, assistance to the working poor to supplement wages leads to "permanent dependency."[47] The Heritage Foundation has extended this opposition to aid for the working poor, claiming that welfare provisions that allow recipients to keep a sizable portion of their outside earnings have failed simply because "recipients who worked remained indefinitely on the welfare rolls."[48] From this perspective work and welfare never mix, and the only legitimate goal of government intervention is total self-sufficiency through work.

The meaning of dependency for those opposed to helping the working poor is illustrated graphically in President Reagan's drive to force the working poor off the welfare rolls. Convinced that all workers should be able to support themselves and their dependents if they try hard enough, the administration has sought to terminate poverty-stricken families from AFDC, thereby ensuring that they do not obtain a "false sense of security" and providing "the incentive to make the transition from welfare to self-support."[49] Throughout the debate on its welfare proposals the Reagan administration has insisted that restricted eligibility and reduced benefit levels would not harm recipients with genuine need, applauding "reductions in dependency" with confidence that those who lost benefits found other means of self-support.

Consistent with the Reagan administration's ideology, 1981 budget cuts in the AFDC and food stamp programs fell heavily on those recipients with earned income, raising marginal tax rates dramatically and rendering some ineligible for federal assistance. As a result of these changes the disposable income of the typical AFDC family with earnings fell in every state in 1982, and in twelve states the impact on work incentives was so severe that a nonworking AFDC parent with two children ended up better off than a working parent in similar circumstances. In California an AFDC recipient realized almost no gain by earning an additional $100 to $350 per month and actually would have lost income at the margin by earning more than $350 through work.[50] Nationwide, the disposable income of the average AFDC working family fell from $595 per month in fiscal 1981 to $476 in 1982 as a result of the Reagan cuts, moving the same average family from 101 percent of the poverty line in 1981 to 81 percent in 1982.[51]

In the wake of President Reagan's welfare cuts many observers predicted that recipients would find it advantageous to quit their jobs and rely solely on welfare for support. Although data on the percentage of terminated recipients returning to the welfare rolls are limited, preliminary evidence suggests that most recipients forced off the rolls have not abandoned work and returned to the welfare system. An exploratory study by the Research Triangle Institute concluded that only 15 percent of those working recipients who lost their benefits in late 1981 and early 1982 had returned several months later to the rolls in the same county in which they had initially enrolled.[52] Richard Nathan similarly found in a survey of selected states that only about 10 percent of those who lost their benefits due to lower income ceilings and altered tax laws have reappeared on the rolls, resulting in a net reduction in the size of the welfare population nationally of 9 percent.[53] A few states have reported higher rates of return, including estimates in the range of 30 to 40 percent in Wisconsin and Oklahoma.[54] However, it appears that most families with earned incomes were able to cope with marginal losses without resorting to complete dependency.

Administration reactions to these findings have rendered its view of dependency unmistakably clear. The White House cited the Research Triangle Institute study as proof that the administration's welfare cuts have been "extremely successful" and that working recipients were "removed from dependency."[55] Because the Reagan philosophy characterizes any contribution to an individual's income through welfare as dependency, the option of gradually phasing out benefits to provide positive incentives for increased work effort is rejected as a matter of principle. The administration policy is not to redefine the inevitable balance between work incentives and targeting; its intent is to eliminate the tradeoff completely by removing from the rolls any person capable of work and by providing assistance only to the deserving poor, giving them as little as possible to ensure that they remain truly needy.

Defendants of Reagan's welfare policies argue that budget cuts weakening work incentives constituted a small portion of total welfare expenditures and that the prior balance between work incentives and targeting of benefits was not sacrosanct. However, the disturbing aspect of the administration's assault on work incentives is that its concept of dependency leaves no room for *any* reasonable mixture of work and welfare to meet the needs of the working poor. Jodie Allen, a Carter administration official and advocate of combining work with welfare, emphasized the extremism embodied in the administration's approach, stating, "If your single criterion for welfare success is saving money, you might as well close all the welfare offices. None of the recipients would then be 'dependent.' Hungry, maybe, but not dependent."[56] Indeed, the Research Triangle Institute investigators questioned the conclusion that the policy could be labeled a success, adding "we cannot say how people coped."[57] Given that the people affected by the Reagan cuts live on the margin of poverty, their impact on the work effort of recipients is in part irrelevant to their merits as sound welfare policy. As Peter Edelman has stressed, an assault on work incentives is counterproductive whether or not recipients continue to work because it will either result in more welfare outlays or require people to work for wages that will bring lower incomes than they received on welfare.[58]

Throughout the past two decades analysts have stressed that the goals of adequate basic benefits, meaningful work incentives, and affordable program costs in federal welfare programs inevitably conflict.[59] Since the 1967 amendments to the Social Security Act—through two Democratic and two Republican administrations—welfare initiatives have recognized the need for compromise among these competing goals and sought to improve previously neglected work incentives. The result of such reforms has been to channel a portion of total welfare benefits to less needy individuals, an outcome that the U.S. Chamber of Commerce has recognized as necessary "in order to provide adequate rewards for those who work and earn."[60] The Reagan administration has reversed this drive toward balance in the targeting of welfare benefits with its unrelenting emphasis on the truly needy.

Societal standards of justice and generosity of course are relative, so it can be argued that the working poor who subsist near the poverty line do not "need" public assistance. Yet to portray recipients affected by Reagan's budget cuts as having comfortable or even adequate incomes is to conceal the true extent of their suffering and sacrifice. Working as hard today as in 1980, the working poor are less able to provide for their families and meet their basic needs. The unwillingness of conservatives to abandon a pathological view of poverty and to allow work and welfare to mix also enhances the difficulties of moving the nonworking poor from the welfare rolls to self-sufficiency.

The lives and experience of the working poor contradict the basic tenet of traditional free market advocates—that poverty stems from lack of motivation and willingness to work. Individuals without earned incomes can be dealt with in straightforward fashion: supported with public funds if unsuited for work and compelled to work if judged capable of self-support. Harsh or rigid determinations are justified with the assumption that work is available at wage levels that will lift the able bodied, sooner or later, out of poverty and dependency. Only the working poor present an anomaly in this otherwise neat explanation of poverty. Perhaps it is for this reason that ideological conservatives have chosen to turn their backs on the working poor, whose struggles and commitment to work most closely approximate the conservative vision of the American dream.

NOTES

1. Ronald Reagan, February 18, 1981.
2. Lester M. Salamon, *Welfare: The Elusive Consensus* (New York: Praeger 1978), p. 66.
3. Bruno Stein, *On Relief: The Economics of Poverty and Public Welfare* (New York: Basic Books, 1981); Frances Fox Piven and Richard Cloward, *Regulating the Poor: The Functions of Public Welfare* (New York: Vintage Books, 1971).
4. Martin Anderson, *Welfare* (Stanford, Cal.: Hoover Institution Press, 1978), p. 162.
5. Leslie Lenkowsky, "Welfare Reform and the Liberals," *Commentary*, March 1979, p. 61.
6. Ronald Reagan, October 12, 1982 and January 21, 1983.
7. Ronald Reagan, September 9, 1982.
8. Milton and Rose Friedman, *Free to Choose* (New York: Harcourt Brace Jovanovich, 1980), p. 108; cited by Ronald Reagan, January 21, 1983.
9. *Budget of the United States Government*, 1984 (Washington, D.C.: U.S. Government Printing Office, 1983), p. M10.
10. Remarks by Edwin Meese to wire service reporters, December 8, 1983.
11. George Gilder, *Wealth and Poverty* (New York: Basic Books, 1981), p. 118.
12. Roger A. Freeman, *The Wayward Welfare State* (Stanford, Cal.: Hoover Institution Press, 1981), pp. 107–8.
13. Ronald Reagan, January 21, 1983.
14. Testimony of David Stockman, director of the Office of Management and Budget, before the Subcommittees on Oversight, and Public Assistance and Unemployment, House Committee on Ways and Means, U.S. Congress, November 3, 1983; *Budget of the United States Government*, 1984 (Washington, D.C.: U.S. Government Printing Office, 1983), pp. 5, 123, 4.
15. James R. Storey, "Income Security," in John L. Palmer and Isabel V. Sawhill, eds., *The Reagan Experiment* (Washington, D.C.: The Urban Institute Press, 1982), pp. 385–86.
16. Spencer Rich, "States and Communities Remain Cool to President's 'Workfare' Programs," *Washington Post*, March 14, 1984.
17. Lawrence M. Mead, "Social Programs and Social Obligations," *Public Interest*, Fall 1982, pp. 27, 28.
18. Martin Anderson, *Welfare*, pp. 162–63.
19. Lester M. Salamon, *Welfare: The Elusive Consensus*, p. 110.
20. Milton and Rose Friedman, *Free to Choose*, p. 98.

21. Martin Anderson, *Welfare*, p. 56.
22. Lawrence M. Mead, "Social Programs and Social Obligations," p. 22.
23. Ken Auletta, "Dependency and Dignity," *New Republic*, February 7, 1983, pp. 33–34.
24. Greg Duncan, et. al., *Years of Poverty, Years of Plenty* (Ann Arbor: University of Michigan, Institute for Social Research, 1984); Leslie Lenkowsky, "Welfare Reform and the Liberals," pp. 60–67.
25. Henry Aaron, *Politics and the Professors* (Washington, D.C.: The Brookings Institution, 1978), p. 36.
26. U.S. Department of Health and Human Services, *1979 AFDC Recipient Characteristics Study—Part 1: Demographic and Program Statistics*, SSA Publication No. 13-11729, June 1982, pp. 27–28.
27. Richard D. Coe, "Welfare Dependency: Fact or Myth?" *Challenge*, September–October 1982, pp. 43–49.
28. U.S. Department of Health and Human Services, *1979 AFDC Recipient Characteristics Study*, pp. 45, 57.
29. Ronald Reagan, December 18, 1982.
30. Ronald Reagan, October 4, 1982.
31. Roger A. Freeman, *The Wayward Welfare State*, p. 25.
32. Ibid.
33. George Gilder, *Wealth and Poverty*, pp. 158, 165–67.
34. Alexander T. Jordan, "The JFK Express," *National Review*, April 17, 1981, p. 420.
35. George Gilder, *Wealth and Poverty*, p. 99.
36. Ibid., p. 66.
37. Ibid., pp. 90–91.
38. Ronald Reagan quoted in Haynes Johnson, "There's More to America Than Just a Horatio Alger Dream," *Washington Post*, July 3, 1983, p. A3, 39. Bradley R. Schiller, "Welfare: Reforming Our Expectations," *Public Interest*, Winter 1981, pp. 60, 64.
40. U.S. Department of Health and Human Services, *1979 AFDC Recipient Characteristics Study*, pp. 48–49.
41. David M. Gordon, *The Working Poor: Towards a State Agenda* (Washington, D.C.: Council of State Planning Agencies, 1979).
42. Bureau of the Census, *Money Income and Poverty Status*, 1982, Series P-60, No. 140 (Washington, D.C.: U.S. Government Printing Office, 1982), p. 4.
43. Sar A. Levitan, Garth L. Mangum, and Ray Marshall, *Human Resources and Labor Markets* (New York: Harper & Row, 1981), pp. 108–20; Michael J. Piore, "Notes for a Theory of Labor Market Stratification," Working Paper No. 95 (Cambridge, Mass.: Massachusetts Institute of Technology, 1972).

44. Michael E. Borus, "Willingness to Work among Youth," *Journal of Human Resources*, Fall 1981, p. 592.
45. Nathan Glazer, "Reform Work, Not Welfare," *Public Interest*, Summer 1975, p. 10.
46. Ronald Reagan, September 15, 1982.
47. Tom Joe and Frank Farrow, "The Eternal Triangle: Work Incentives, Welfare and the Poor," *Jobs Watch*, February 1983, p. 10.
48. Cited in "Conservative-Liberal Battle on Welfare," *Socioeconomic Newsletter*, Institute for Socioeconomic Studies, March–April 1983, p. 6.
49. Statement of Linda S. McMahon, associate commissioner for family assistance before the U.S. Congress, House Budget Committee, December 14, 1982 (in press).
50. Tom Joe and Frank Farrow, "The Eternal Triangle," p. 9.
51. James R. Storey, "Income Security," p. 384; Tom Joe, "Profiles of Families in Poverty: Effects of the 1982 Budget Proposals on the Poor" (Washington, D.C.: Center for the Study of Social Policy, February 1982).
52. Linda E. Demkovich, "Rosy Reading of Working Poor Study Miffs Researchers," *National Journal*, May 7, 1983, pp. 975–76.
53. Richard P. Nathan, "The Underclass Challenges the Social Sciences," *Wall Street Journal*, July 8, 1983, p. 20.
54. "Effects of Federal AFDC Policy Changes: A Study of a Federal–State 'Partnership' " (Washington, D.C.: Center for the Study of Social Policy, March 1983), pp. 74–76.
55. Jodie T. Allen, "Welfare Cutbacks: No Success Story," *Washington Post*, May 4, 1983, p. A27.
56. Ibid.
57. Linda E. Demkovich, "Rosy Reading," p. 976.
58. Peter Edelman, "Work and Welfare: An Alternative Perspective on Entitlements," *Budget and Policy Choices 1983* (Washington, D.C.: Center for National Policy, 1983), p. 53.
59. James Tobin, "The Case for an Income Guarantee," *Public Interest*, Summer 1966, pp. 37, 39; Henry J. Aaron, *Why Is Welfare So Hard to Reform?* (Washington, D.C.: The Brookings Institution, 1973), pp. 68–69; Frederick Doolittle, Frank Levy, and Michael Wiseman, "The Mirage of Welfare Reform," *Public Interest*, Spring 1977, pp. 63, 77; Martin Anderson, *Welfare*, pp. 133–51.
60. U.S. Chamber of Commerce, *High Employment and Income Maintenance Policy: A Report of the Council on Trends and Perspectives* (Washington, D.C.: Chamber of Commerce of the United States, 1976), p. 52.

3

Hindrance Instead of Help

*Conservatives surely, above all, have long
known and warned that real poverty is less a
state of income than a state of mind and that
the government dole blights most of the people
who come to depend on it. The lesson of the
period since 1964—a lesson so manifest it
cannot be gainsaid—is that conservatives, if
anything, understated their argument.*[1]

—George Gilder

Having made the claim that the poor suffer deprivation by
choice, or at least by virtue of their own inadequacies,
opponents of government assistance in aid of the poor also
develop what they view as a logical corollary—that federal
efforts to help the poor are counterproductive. Conservatives
address the effectiveness of federal interventions with considerable caution, for in so doing they abandon the high
ground of moral absolutes provided by assertions that the
poor do not deserve our help. Yet, to the extent that the
American public remains convinced that some groups do
deserve federal support, advocates of laissez faire can resist
the growth of the welfare state only by challenging the efficacy
of public action. The result is a recurring theme: we cannot
assist the poor even if they need our aid, for federal
interventions inevitably constitute a hindrance instead of a
help.

Underlying the conclusion that federal antipoverty efforts are counterproductive is the assumption that poverty is a function of moral deviance. Conservatives argue that government interventions are harmful by definition in that they weaken links between individual behavior and income among groups already plagued by an inadequate sense of personal responsibility. Other unintended results of federal action are less obvious but allegedly no less threatening to the welfare of the poor and to the total social fabric. Public assistance presumably destroys families and communities, inhibits individual advancement, hinders broader economic growth, and weakens the capacity of state, local, and private agencies to provide for the truly needy. Throughout such assaults on federal intervention welfare programs are portrayed as a threat to the nation's moral fiber and a disruption of the propitious functioning of private markets and local governance.

These diverse attacks on antipoverty initiatives are not easily discredited in that they rarely address the narrow and immediate results of federal intervention. Instead, conservatives contend that federal efforts to aid the poor undermine their moral character and trigger destructive long-term changes in basic social and economic institutions—changes that outweigh any short-term benefits enjoyed by program participants. These criticisms rest heavily upon assertions of causal relationships not readily subject to empirical test. The critiques often embody some element of truth, but their relevance to the net effectiveness of government aid to the poor depends on subtler questions of degree, further complicating the task of rebuttal. Nonetheless, a careful analysis of conservative assumptions—that poverty is a moral problem, that social and economic structures are dramatically altered by antipoverty efforts, and that federal initiatives merely displace more effective state or local public and private programs —reveal that they are sharply at odds with both historical evidence and the findings of contemporary research.

POVERTY AS A MORAL PROBLEM

If poverty is defined as the lack of an adequate income, the federal government obviously has the capacity to reduce or eliminate it. However, if poverty is recast as a moral condition rather than a standard of income inadequacy, it may well prove impervious to government action. Conservatives offer numerous reasons for minimizing the redistributive impact of federal tax and spending policies. Their first line of defense is the claim that government aid cannot help the poor because poverty is a cultural and moral problem rather than an economic one.

In portraying poverty as a moral problem, conservatives view the poor as plagued by behavioral disorders that shape and define their condition. Crime, delinquency, and other social problems are cited as evidence of moral deviance among the poor which cannot be redressed through income transfers. One welfare critic, troubled by the "decline in civility" among the poor and assigning responsibility for this trend to federal antipoverty efforts, concluded that "more than any further economic resource, the disadvantaged now need a more secure sense of order in themselves and the neighborhoods around them . . . . The problem is now more a *moral* one than an economic one, and so is the challenge facing the welfare state."[2] George Gilder makes the argument explicit by claiming that "redistribution cannot fight poverty" and warning that acceptance of "self-indulgent" lower-class behavior will assign the recipients of aid "to permanent poverty, erode the requirements of growth and opportunity, and foster processes of cultural and economic deterioration."[3]

The grains of truth in these descriptions of poverty are evident. Income redistribution can bring only modest gains if unaccompanied by meaningful initiatives to expand the poor's opportunities for work, self-sufficiency, and control of their destiny. Because greater progress has been made in developing a system of income transfers than in broadening employment opportunities for the poor or advancing their political clout, the lack of future prospects remains a key aspect of poverty in America. These facts can be accepted without believing that poverty is a moral problem—that is, that poverty stems primarily from the deviant character and behavior of the poor. These findings also do not contradict the pressing need of those in poverty for additional income and the effectiveness of federal welfare programs in placing an income floor beneath those facing abject deprivation.

By emphasizing the imagined moral causes of poverty, opponents of government intervention deftly seek to shift attention away from the economic plight that is shared by all the poor toward an idealized image of individual responsibility. The tone and substance of such arguments imply that welfare benefits are irrelevant as a response to poverty and that government is actually impeding the self-reliance that alone can resolve a moral problem:

> Time and time again, government has perpetuated a problem that would have solved itself long ago if there had been no interference, because the individuals involved would have seen no alternative but to get their own hands dirty and take care of the matter themselves.
>
> The rejection of personal responsibility for an undesired turn of events, the outward projection of what often is the result of the individual's inadequate concern, planning, precaution, preparation, effort or plain neglect or unwillingness to face unpleasant facts, expresses the spirit of a wayward welfare state.[4]

The curious presumption that federal intervention has not reduced poverty ignores incontrovertible data on the subject. Nonetheless, because conservatives are preoccupied with the behavioral problems and presumed moral deviance of the poor, the true causes of poverty are ignored.

Another variant of the view of poverty as a moral problem presents loss of dignity as a more onerous fate than material deprivation. According to Ronald Reagan, welfare is one of our major problems because it destroys "self-reliance, dignity and self-respect . . . the very substance of moral fibre."[5]

The alternative has been termed "earned dignity" or "dignity of achievement"—the dignity that is obtained when one achieves "that modest well-being presumed within the grasp of honest effort" and that is meaningful only if accompanied by censure of failure and "a strong sense of the shameful."[6] The poor are faced with a no-win situation: reliance on welfare precludes a sense of dignity, and yet failure to earn a decent income also must invoke censure and shame. In this view dignity can be found only in self-sufficiency through work or inheritance, a goal that is out of reach for millions of the working and dependent poor.

Granting the virtues of personal responsibility and dignity, the question is whether any attempt to alleviate the economic problems of the poor necessarily destroys these qualities and worsens their plight. In the absence of efforts to enhance employability and earnings capacity, income transfers certainly can undermine recipients' sense of dignity and responsibility. Yet when coupled with appropriate initiatives to expand economic opportunity, income support can extend a helping hand to the poor while bolstering self-sufficiency and concomitant self-respect. Conservatives overlook this vital distinction between policies that destroy self-esteem and those that give it a chance to flourish. To help is to hurt, they argue, and therefore the poor are best left to their own devices—albeit poor, but retaining as much of a sense of responsibility and dignity as their failures will allow.

In casting poverty as a moral problem, conservatives also ignore the tangible ways in which federal initiatives have succeeded in reducing deprivation in America. Largely as a result of the antipoverty programs launched in the 1960s, the official poverty rate fell from 22.2 percent in 1960 to a low of 11.4 percent in 1978, and in-kind assistance further eased the hardship suffered by the poor. Since 1978 this decline has been reversed and the poverty rate has risen by more than one-third in four years, a result of retrenchments in government aid, inflation, and high unemployment. Notwithstanding this setback, however, federal aid has enabled millions of households to secure their basic needs, carrying the poor through difficult times and giving them a chance to look to the future.

Despite increasing federal expenditures for programs in aid of the poor, progress in combating poverty has been impeded by a diverse set of developments. Rapid escalation in housing and energy prices in the 1970s hit the poor especially hard, and slack labor markets lessened the opportunities of impoverished Americans to improve their fortunes through work. Efforts to reduce poverty have also been hampered by a sharp rise in the number of female-headed, single-parent households—a trend that opponents of government inter-vention have seized upon as evidence that federal antipoverty programs destroy the family and exacerbate the moral problem of poverty. The role of social programs in the dissolution of low-income families has emerged as a subject of intense debate, for a strong causal relationship between welfare and family breakups is a central component of the claim that federal aid to the poor is counterproductive.

FAMILIES IN POVERTY

The charge that provision of income to the poor destroys families typically elicits strong emotional reactions. Evoking images of an intrusive state disrupting an otherwise tranquil family nest, federal welfare programs take on a sinister quality. Already suspicious of the moral character of the poor, the nonpoor majority find it easy to accept the notion that their less fortunate neighbors are unable to manage their personal lives or to make reasonable decisions regarding the future of their families. The causal relationships between poverty and family instability, and the net effect of income assistance and family dissolution on the broader well-being of poor indi-viduals, rarely receive careful attention.

Assertions of a direct link between increases in federal social welfare expenditures and the proliferation of low-income, single-parent families have become commonplace in contemporary conservative thought. Milton and Rose Friedman blithely accept the conclusion that welfare programs weaken the family and "rot the moral fabric that holds a decent society together."[7] Considering the family to be "the only institution capable of generating upward mobility," George Gilder contends that social programs have brought "a great increase in the incomes of the poor in America at the cost of the catastrophic breakdown of their families."[8] President Reagan has placed this litany at the core of his administration's social policies, unabashedly stating that "there is no question that many well-intentioned Great Society-type programs contributed to family breakups, welfare dependency and a large increase in births out of wedlock."[9]

Regardless of its cause the trend toward single-parent, female-headed households, popularly termed the feminization of poverty, clearly enhances the difficulty of combating poverty in the United States. Two-parent families are far less likely to suffer poverty—only one in thirteen are poor, compared to one in three families headed by a female—while many female heads of households have no hope of earning enough to lift their families out of poverty even if they are able to obtain full-time work.[10] The rise of single-parent families is particularly significant as an obstacle to economic progress among blacks. Virtually half of black households are headed by single women, and their low earnings capacity has completely offset relative income gains by other types of black families over the past two decades.[11]

The decline of two-parent families among the poor poses a serious obstacle to antipoverty efforts, but it is by no means clear that federal programs in aid of the poor have played a major role in promoting family dissolution. It is a fact that increases in social expenditures and in the number of single-parent families occurred during roughly the same period. Conservatives are quick to correlate the two phenomena, assuming that welfare benefits and regulations govern the lives of the poor.

One of the few detailed accounts of how federal social programs affect interpersonal relations within low-income families (a version in many ways unrepresentative of conservative orthodoxy regarding the family) is offered by George Gilder. His graphic explanation speaks for itself:

> Marriages dissolve not because the rules dictate it, but because the benefit levels destroy the father's key role and authority.
>
> Nothing is so destructive of . . . male values as the growing, impervious recognition that when all is said and done his wife and children can do better without him. The man has a gradually sinking feeling that his role as provider, the definitive male activity from the primal days of the hunt through the industrial revolution and on into modern life, has been largely seized from him; he has been cuckolded by the compassionate state.
>
> His response to this reality is that very combination of resignation and rage, escapism and violence, short horizons and promiscuous sexuality that characterizes everywhere the life of the poor.[12]

Basing his argument on this extraordinary blend of chauvinism and social history, Gilder concludes that the expansion of welfare since 1964 has left behind "a wreckage of broken lives and families worse than the aftermath of slavery," particularly among blacks. He also claims that the "fact that they have more income only makes the situation less remediable."[13]

Besides his bizarre presentation of male sexuality and motivation, Gilder's explanation of the link between public assistance and family dissolution is based on highly selective data and held together by unsubstantiated logic. While Gilder portrays the inability of husband and father to provide for his family as central to the disintegration of marriages, he fails to acknowledge the extent to which the inadequacies of the labor market contribute to this frustration. Whatever sense of personal failure accompanies the inability to support one's family, it certainly would be at least as powerful if the family lived in abject poverty as in welfare dependency—the obvious difference being that the secure income of welfare heightens the potential independence of wife and mother under such adverse circumstances. Yet in Gilder's view all members of low-income families would be better off if welfare payments were withheld, for while they might have less income the male heads of households would still retain their pride, thereby fostering the preservation of stable marriages.

Gilder's argument runs the risk of all theories unsubstantiated by empirical evidence: that causal relationships that seem plausible will prove nonexistent. He relies heavily on the claim that welfare is the primary source of humiliation and destructive behavior, allowing a poor man's family to do better without him. But research data have failed to support this account of family dissolution. An Urban Institute study found that most female heads of households on welfare attributed their separations from husbands or boyfriends to personal rather than economic factors and that the primary effect of welfare on women heading families was to reduce pressures to remarry rather than to provide incentives for separation.[14] Similarly, a report prepared for the congressional Joint Economic Committee estimated that 36 percent of the increase in female-headed households between 1950 and 1972 could have been attributed to the movement of existing female-headed families out of the households of parents or relatives rather than additions to the number of female-headed families through family dissolution.[15] The negative income tax experiments in Seattle and Denver found that the rate of marital dissolution among recipients increased despite the availability of payments to two-parent families and a graduated tax structure that ensured that low-income mothers would not be better off without the presence and earnings of their husbands.[16] Rather than claim a causal effect, it would be more correct to argue that assistance to low-income families produces an "independence effect," allowing greater choice in establishing separate households outside marriage.

Ironically, in the past it has been the desire of conservatives seeking to restrict assistance to the deserving poor that has had the effect of establishing perverse incentives for able-bodied males to abandon their families in order to ensure a subsistence income for their wives and children. Nonetheless, nearly half the states, accounting for roughly 70 percent of all AFDC recipients, have qualified unemployed fathers to receive welfare payments, thus eliminating the obvious impetus for the creation of female-headed households from the welfare system. Still, in some undefined way it is suggested that public assistance dictates the behavior of the poor and is responsible for the dissolution of families. Closer to the truth is the realization that welfare rules do not dictate the family decisions of the poor but that adequate benefits may offer them the opportunity to act on their own needs and desires.

The strains that low wages and deprivation place on families living in poverty are factors in family dissolution that conservatives generally choose to ignore. Considerable evidence suggests that the adequacy of male and female wage rates have had a far greater impact on the growth of female-headed households than has the level of welfare benefits. While a 10 percent increase in AFDC benefits was linked to a 2 percent rise in female-headed families, a comparable jump in female wage rates was accompanied by a 7 percent increase in such families. Furthermore, a 10 percent increase in male wage rates was associated with an 8 percent decline in female family heads.[17] The implication is clear: improvements in the earnings of men in poor families will lessen financial strains and reduce the attractiveness of female-headed families, while enhanced income prospects for poor women (through work or welfare) will bolster their ability to maintain separate households and escape difficult marriages.

Those who choose to view welfare or other aid to the poor as disruptive of the family focus on the fact that broken marriages and single-parent families make it more difficult to escape poverty, ignoring the fact that poverty tends to break up families. Psychologist James Comer attributes the withdrawal of impoverished black men from family and work to a growing sense of futility. He states that "in a society where the male is supposed to be the breadwinner . . . it's a tremendous psychological burden when you know you don't have a snowball's chance in hell of taking care of your family. One of the defenses is not to care, to not do, not try."[18] When trapped in poverty, the familial relationships of the poor are severely tested, all too often falling victim to battered self-esteem.

Finally, although conservatives would like to presume that few societal changes beyond an increase in antipoverty efforts could account for trends in family dissolution, competing explanations and contributing factors abound. Welfare critics are correct in noting that the rise of female-headed households has appeared more sharply among the poor. However, the weakening of religious and communal ties, the loosening of sexual mores, and the greater acceptability of marital separation and divorce over the past two decades have fueled an increase in the number of single-parent families in all income groups. The decline of the traditional family is an irreversible result of social change in an increasingly affluent society, one that will have to be accepted and considered in the development of new strategies to alleviate poverty in the United States.

Decisions about marriage and work are vital choices that shape the course of one's life. There is no reason to suspect that the poor value a reliable spouse or family ties any less than do the nonpoor. The availability of welfare benefits may expand the options open to the poor, giving recipients the means to end a bad marriage. Certainly when possible, fathers should be forced to support their children, as legislation approved by Congress in 1983 provides, so that divorce does not become a means of escaping financial responsibility for one's dependents. Amid these difficult realities, however, it is not credible to argue that federal social programs alone have governed the lives of the poor and been responsible for the deterioration of their families.

STIFLING THE ENGINES OF GROWTH

Opponents of welfare view the deterioration of low-income families as the major moral threat posed by federal aid to the poor. They also contend that government intervention creates poverty and destroys opportunity by diminishing the economy's potential for growth, thereby restricting upward mobility. Claims of government's counterproductive role rest both on the alleged misallocation of resources to nonproductive endeavors and on the presumed costs of social regulation. The underlying assumptions are that the free labor market is the most efficient distributor of opportunity based on merit and that the lot of the poor would improve if the federal government ceased to interfere.

Moving from the premise that the market's allocation of resources maximizes efficiency and growth, those committed to laissez faire principles necessarily conclude that federal spending to expand opportunity can only subvert that goal. As expressed in the Reagan administration's initial economic recovery program,

> federal programs have thus been created and expanded in the name of stimulating growth, jobs . . . and in other ways to alter and finetune the level and composition of national economic activity. Many of these programs, however, have served to distort the market economy and have thereby contributed as much to the problems they were intended to address as to their solution.[19]

Even in cases where opportunity and self-sufficiency are increased through federal efforts, conservatives contend that the benefits are outweighed by the diminished growth and inflationary pressures that accompany social welfare expenditures. For some, social programs are inherently wasteful and inflationary because they divert resources from productive endeavors in the private market. For others, the danger lies in an excessive commitment to insatiable social welfare demands, requiring prudent limits on federal social programs despite evidence of unmet needs. Regardless of the rationale weakened economic performance is deemed sufficiently harmful to negate the beneficial results of federal intervention in aid of the needy.

If the link between social welfare expenditures and poor economic performance is accepted, the rejection of government assistance can rest solely on the assumption that economic growth and price stability will help improve the economic status of the poor. Michael Novak presented precisely this argument as a moral justification for Reaganomics, claiming that

> the Reagan economic plan is based upon a diagnosis of the 'upward push' of the poor and lower-income classes, who seek upward mobility. The only hope such persons have for upward mobility lies in (a) a growing, innovative, investment-rich economy and (b) the containment of inflation. Unless inflation is contained, the progress of lower-income families is virtually impossible. Upward push stops when the economy stops growing and when its industrial plant becomes obsolete. A society which loses economic dynamism cannot offer hope to families of lower income.[20]

President Reagan has offered similar justifications for cuts in social spending and inaction amid sharply rising unemployment. Claiming that poor families have gained additional purchasing power through its anti-inflation efforts, the Reagan administration has argued that low-income Americans benefit more from reduced inflation and accelerated growth than from direct aid and that it is not possible to have both. In the administration's words, "the Federal Government can do more to provide lasting assistance to the disadvantaged by assuring strong and less inflationary economic growth than through income transfer programs."[21]

The 1983 *Economic Report of the President,* prepared while joblessness reached its postwar peak, reflects the strength of the philosophical bias against federal programs to expand employment and broaden economic opportunity. Although it voiced support for training to assist the structurally unemployed, the report implicitly rejected the job creation proposals of "well-meaning" members of Congress with the statement that "only a balanced and lasting recovery can achieve a substantial reduction in unemployment."[22] In addition the report was highly critical of public works projects to boost employment, contending that they generally are poorly timed, displace or delay state and local expenditures, crowd out private sector employment, and offer little benefit to the unemployed. The only proposed responses to what the report labeled "the most serious economic problem now facing the United States" was a modest training program for displaced workers and other long-term unemployed and revisions in federal unemployment insurance statutes that would allow states to use unemployment insurance funds for training, job-search assistance, and wage subsidies.[23]

Throughout his political career President Reagan has opposed federal job creation programs, arguing that they generate unproductive work and weaken the national economy. With a litany of references to "make-work jobs" and "quick fix" responses to recession, his administration has portrayed public employment initiatives as dismal failures that led to long-term economic decline. Even when the unemployment rate reached double-digit figures in September 1982, the president offered the following accounts of federal public works and other jobs programs:

> Public works jobs programs have proven to be expensive failures. They were the things that for seven previous recessions the Government has turned to, and it was like a quick fix—stimulated the economy briefly but about two years later you fell into another recession. And every one of them was deeper and worse than the one before. Now they'd [liberals] drag us right back with that kind of program into the swamp that we've been trying so hard to lift ourselves out of.[24]

Actually, what we're talking about is building a solid base for the economy as the method of providing the jobs the unemployed need, and providing them on a more or less permanent basis instead of just a quick flurry that does no real good but leaves us closer to the brink of disaster than we were before.[25]

Reagan's assessment of the much-maligned federal employment and training program was similar. He has charged that public service employment created "jobs without any future" and that training efforts left participants unsuited for jobs in the private sector.[26]

The "trickle down" theory that the poor are best served by anti-inflation and growth-oriented strategies has a long history. For this tactic to meet the test of social justice it is not necessary that those with low incomes reap the greatest gains or even that all income groups share its benefits equally. It simply must be shown that other federal policies would be less effective in promoting the well-being of the poor. As proponents frequently acknowledge, "some Americans will surely do less well than others, but everyone does eventually gain" when demands on government are reduced "to allow the economy to perform, albeit imperfectly, its traditional role of increasing the welfare of all Americans."[27] The relative fairness of this approach ultimately depends upon the accuracy of conservative claims that federal social welfare interventions are incompatible with stable prices and economic growth.

By identifying federal spending as the cause of stagflation and labeling defense expenditures as essential to national security, conservatives have sought to forge a direct link between social welfare programs, budget deficits, and the nation's economic ills. In the extreme, huge federal deficits can push interest rates upward, thereby fueling inflation and dampening economic growth. However, social expenditures represent one of several components of the federal budget, and numerous combinations of tax and spending policies can yield deficits within manageable levels. As Ben Wattenberg has stressed, the unprecedented prosperity of the past thirty years has coincided with the rise of the welfare state, a development its critics generally choose to ignore.[28] These parallel trends in economic growth and federal intervention may be coincidental, but they belie the claim that prosperity and social justice are mutually exclusive.

The Reagan administration has exaggerated the dangers posed by federal deficits when assaulting social programs while recklessly ignoring those threats in its defense and tax policies. The rapid growth of entitlement expenditures throughout the 1970s lent credence to the argument that social spending lay at the heart of the persistent deficit problem. By 1983 that causal relationship was rejected by President Reagan's chairman of the Council of Economic Advisers, Martin Feldstein, who argued that an unprecedented defense buildup and tax reduction were "driving the deficit." With federal deficits projected to exceed $200 billion annually throughout this decade, and with defense expenditures under Reagan consuming an ever-larger portion of the projected federal budget, the impact of federal aid to the poor on the nation's broader economic health is far less certain than conservatives generally imply.

While federal deficits have swelled to mammoth proportions during Reagan's first three years, spending for social programs has fallen considerably. Between 1980 and 1984, the shares of the total federal budget devoted to nondefense discretionary programs and means-tested entitlement for low-income Americans declined by roughly 25 percent. President Reagan has cut $26 billion from 19 federal programs designed to provide aid to the nation's poor, and he proposes to spend a smaller percentage of GNP on means-tested and discretionary programs in 1989 than was allocated for these purposes at the inception of the Great Society in 1965. His administration's massive deficits may jeopardize future economic growth, but spending for social programs clearly is not responsible for the rising tide of red ink. Even if *all* discretionary spending—for education, nutrition, pollution control, health centers, employment and training, and so on—was eliminated by 1988, the federal deficit would still exceed $70 billion.

Federal social welfare programs can also be equated with large deficits and poor economic performance only if conservative assumptions about American tax burdens are accepted. Acknowledging the need for increased defense expenditures in the near future, there is no need to choose between federal efforts to reduce poverty and responsible fiscal policy. In 1980, prior to the sweeping Reagan tax cuts adopted in 1981, the combined receipts of all levels of government totaled 30.7 percent of the nation's gross domestic product (GDP). In contrast, 42.6 percent of GDP was devoted to government functions in France, 37.4 percent in West Germany, and 32.9 percent in Canada. Similarly, Western European nations spend far more proportionally for social welfare programs than the United States. These countries are frequently cited as challenging America's predominant position in international markets, and yet they support a tax burden at least as great as any found in the United States.

Economic trends since enactment of the Reagan tax cuts have failed to substantiate the potential returns advocates claimed for the reduced tax burdens. Most notably, the tax cuts have not produced the surge in savings and investment which played a key role in supply-side theories. While the old-fashioned Keynesian medicine of deficit spending fueled economic recovery in 1983–1984, the pattern of the past four years provides no support for conservative assumptions of a direct link between tax burdens prior to 1980 and sluggish economic growth.

The prospects of the poor are diminished by slow rates of economic growth both because aid to them is reduced and because their living standards can be seriously eroded during periods of rapid inflation. Yet there is little reason to believe that general prosperity offers a substitute for the assistance provided through targeted employment and income transfer programs. At best, the poor appear to benefit proportionately from long-term economic growth, and among the most disadvantaged low-income groups the returns are likely to be more meager.[29] In contrast, targeted employment policies have been found to generate substantially greater benefits for the poor than have tax reductions or other strategies for broad economic stimulus.[30] To the extent that prosperity does not reach many of the needy who cannot compete effectively in the labor market, federal intervention to expand economic opportunity is essential.

Given the goal of broadening economic opportunity for the poor, it is ironic that conservatives reserve some of their harshest criticism for federal employment initiatives. Critics of federal jobs programs raise some valid concerns—past efforts have suffered under multiple objectives and political pressures, have often been implemented too lat to be effective as a countercyclical measure, and have been developed too hurriedly to promote careful targeting or sound administration of federal funds. Yet available evidence suggests that carefully drafted programs with adequate financial support can be successful in imparting valuable work experience and open opportunities to low-income Americans. Without federal aid the most disadvantaged have little chance of sharing in the fruits of prosperity and the increased economic opportunities it might bring.

Opponents of federal intervention attempt to reconcile their laissez faire philosophy with a commitment to expanded economic opportunity by casting government as the obstacle to individual and societal advance. In another example of Orwellian "doublespeak," President Reagan kicked off his reelection effort with appeals to "our bold vision of an opportunity society for the future," one which seeks to "bring out the best in every person, because we know every man and woman carries the spark of greatness."[32] While sounding distinctly liberal, his prescriptions implied that only the meddling habits of liberals and federal bureaucrats limit the horizons of the poor and disadvantaged. Arguing that opportunity is limited by government-imposed barriers to economic growth, Reagan returned to the usual litany of appeals for lower taxes, reduced government intervention, and a return to traditional values as the key to extending opportunity to all Americans.

Perhaps the most frequently cited example of how government limits opportunity and creates poverty is that favorite conservative whipping boy, the minimum wage. Critics of federal minimum wage legislation contend that recent increases have priced many low-skilled workers, particularly minority and teenage jobseekers, out of the labor market. While the federal minimum wage remains too low to lift many families out of poverty even when full-time work is available, its opponents believe that a sizable number of the unemployed in poor households would gain access to earned income in the absence of a statutory minimum wage.

Research attempts to measure accurately the relationship between a statutory wage floor and aggregate employment levels have been inconclusive and often contradictory. The implications of lowering or eliminating the minimum wage are particularly difficult to assess because this wage protection has become inextricably intertwined with the nation's social welfare system. While continuing to fulfill its original function of preventing rampant wage exploitation, the minimum wage also remains the most direct and comprehensive policy tool to improve the lot of the working poor. An excessively narrow focus on the probable elimination of some jobs obscures these broader benefits of a federal minimum wage.

At the current federal minimum hourly rate a wage earner working full time and year round with two dependents still remains in poverty. Moreover, few jobs in the secondary labor market, where most low-wage workers are concentrated, are stable enough to ensure full-time, full-year employment. For these workers the federal minimum wage remains the last line of defense before slipping into abject poverty. Elimination of the wage floor, favored by many conservatives, would undoubtedly save a few more jobs but would also swell the ranks of the impoverished. Required to pay a minimum wage, some employers may be encouraged to invest more in the training of their workers, thus raising productivity and enhancing those workers' employability and self-sufficiency.

For prospective workers the federal minimum wage provides an incentive to rely on earnings rather than on welfare. Torn between the known benefits of dependency and the risks of an unstable job market, these workers are more likely to choose the latter if the money reward is sufficiently high. Eliminating the minimum wage, or lowering it to an ineffective level, would reduce work incentive and make welfare the more attractive alternative. A society that places a high value on the work ethic should also be willing to pay a price for inducing the poor to work.

The benefits of recent proposals to lower the minimum wage to increase job prospects among unemployed youth are similarly limited. In loose labor markets such a program may have the effect of drawing students out of school and displacing older workers to fill newly created jobs. Solving the problem of youth unemployment by lowering the minimum wage provides a mixed blessing for the poor; any advantages for the young may be gained at the expense of their elders.[32]

DESTROYING PRIVATE INITIATIVE

The claim that government intervention in aid of the poor is counterproductive—undermining morality, perpetuating poverty, destroying jobs, and weakening economic performance—is bolstered by invoking the images of voluntarism in America. Conservatives argue that federal programs diminish opportunities for the poor by stifling efforts of private institutions to aid low-income persons in more constructive ways. Just as the private market would provide jobs and opportunity if unencumbered by government interference they claim, private charities and local communities would combine to meet the needs of the deserving poor if not preempted by federal actions. Contending that they do not lack compassion, true believers in laissez faire insist that their opposition to federal aid is based on efficiency considerations. Federal initiatives, they assert, simply get in the way of cost-effective aid to the poor.

The Reagan administration has frequently appealed to voluntarism in defending its reduced social welfare efforts. Rewriting the nation's social history, President Reagan portrayed the era prior to substantial federal involvement in social welfare as one without serious social problems, charging that "this Federal Government of ours, by trying to do too much, has undercut the ability of individual people, communities, churches, and businesses to meet the real needs of society as Americans always have met them in the past."[33] He perceives the federal bureaucracy as having intruded into the affairs of state and local governments and displaced the efforts of communities to resolve their own problems:

> We need only to believe in ourselves and to remember that the true strength of this country lies in the minds, the motivation, and the faith of people like yourselves, not the bureaucracy in Washington, D.C. . . . . [T]here are just some areas where the Government has been trying to do things that the Government was never set up to do, and those things belong back here in your States and in your communities.[34]

> The truth is that we've let government take away many things we once considered were really ours to do voluntarily.[35]

Reagan's appeals to voluntary and community action, reflecting nostalgic yearnings for the past that lie at the core of conservative philosophy, presume that private organizations can respond adequately to most social problems and that the proliferation of federal roles and responsibilities has led to the erosion of community in modern America.

The theoretical underpinnings of the Reagan administration's approach to private nonprofit organizations can be traced back to the writings of Edmund Burke.[36] In a modern context sociologist Robert Nisbet has argued that government interventions accelerate the decline of community cohesion and weaken "intermediate associations" between the individual and the state. According to Nisbet the disintegration of community ties and institutions in modern industrial society has been caused by the expansion of government power:

> The conflict between the central power of the political state and the whole set of functions and authorities contained in church, family, guild, and local community has been, I believe, the main source of those dislocations of social structure and uprootings of status which lie behind the problem of community in our age.[37]

Thus, the present-day disciples of Burke argue that government, rather than compensating for the slackening bonds of community, has been primarily responsible for the presumed deterioration of those traditional ties.

The reverse causality proposed by Nisbet has been embraced enthusiastically by conservatives for two reasons. First, this reasoning implies that reductions in government power and interference will halt the destruction of community linkages and perhaps rejuvenate private initiatives directed toward social problems. Second, to the extent that stable and closely knit communities can be shown to contribute to the upward mobility of the poor, Nisbet's view suggests that federal intervention is detrimental to their long-term interests. Gilder speaks for numerous critics of federal social welfare policies who charge that "egalitarian" federal programs destroy the strong communities and familial cultures on which upward mobility depends.[38] Conservative assumptions lead directly to the conclusion that federal programs in aid of the poor are more hindrance than help.

A parallel but narrower argument against government social welfare efforts focuses on the impact of such intervention on private charity. It is based on the claim that expanded government activity hampers the operations of voluntary agencies by competing for clients and labor, restricting the scope and nature of private services and diminishing the perceived need for charitable contributions.[39]

Welfare critic Martin Anderson concludes that because "government, at all levels, has taken a greater and greater role in welfare, people seem to have become more reluctant to contribute to private charitable institutions."[40] Implicit in these attacks is the belief that government programs have merely displaced prior private efforts and that the withdrawal of federal aid would result in no net loss, and possibly a net gain, of resources available to combat the nation's social problems.

Many of these presumed relationships between government intervention and local initiative are too broad to be assessed objectively. By their nature family and community structures evolve in response to myriad social and economic forces. The expansion of government responsibilities may have contributed to a weakening of familial and communal ties, yet federal intervention has responded to powerful societal changes. Trends in geographic mobility, per capita real income, and the secularization of American culture have all influenced the disintegration of extended families and organic communities; the expansion of government responsibilities has been more a reflection of these trends than a cause of resulting changes in family and community life.

In historical accounts of private initiative and charitable giving the conservative thesis appears more clearly at odds with the record. Prior to government intervention private voluntary activities managed to provide only the most modest relief and assistance to portions of the poor population. These efforts were least effective in areas with high concentrations of low-income households and seldom moved beyond the provision of minimal temporary aid to improve the poor's prospects for self-support. The inadequacy of private help, if not its complete breakdown, generated the need for government intervention under the New Deal. As government responded to unmet basic needs there is no convincing evidence that charitable contributions suffered a corresponding decline. Ample evidence suggests that government social welfare efforts have not dampened private giving and that charitable activities may receive greater private support when supplemented by public expenditures.[41] No doubt the focus of private initiatives has shifted as government has accepted responsibility for the provision of basic needs, but the activities of a healthy nonprofit sector still complement government efforts to fulfill pressing social needs. Indeed, the progressive tax structure has encouraged much of the charitable giving during the past four decades.

Administration claims that cuts in federal social welfare expenditures would be offset by an increase in charitable donations to nonprofit agencies have no empirical basis. To make up for the $35 billion lost as a result of Reagan budget policies during fiscal years 1982–85, private voluntary contributions would have to quadruple over prior levels of giving. At the same time, however, the purses of potential donors may have been tightened because personal income tax cuts passed at President Reagan's insistence had the effect of raising the potential costs of charitable contributions.[42] Despite perceptions of increased need, expectations of a dramatic jump in charitable donations hardly seem realistic.

To examine the impact of Reagan budget cuts in greater detail, the Urban Institute has conducted an exhaustive survey of some 6,900 nonprofit organizations throughout the nation and compiled detailed information regarding their financial health. Preliminary data suggest that private agencies have suffered considerably as a result of the administration's social welfare philosophy. The study found that federal, state, and local governments are the largest source of funding for nonprofit organizations, providing approximately 39 percent of their 1982 revenues. Of the organizations receiving this support, 57 percent reported reductions as a consequence of recent federal budget cuts; only 8 percent could claim increases. The remaining 35 percent with no cuts suffered a real decline in the value of their support, which was eroded by inflation. Organizations primarily concerned with the arts and cultural activities escaped relatively unscathed, but significantly reduced government support was reported by 68 percent of those organizations engaged in employment and training, 72 percent of legal services groups, and 62 percent of social service agencies.[43]

Empirical evidence casts considerable doubt on the proposition that federal social welfare expenditures are crowding out private charity. The Urban Institute finding that two-thirds of the existing nonprofit organizations have been founded since 1960 and flourished during a period of rapid government expansion runs counter to conservative claims. The proportion of Americans willing to volunteer some portion of their time in service to others has also increased during the past two decades. The few studies that have examined government expenditures and volunteer effort in areas of higher education and social welfare have found no clear or significant relationship between these two factors.[44]

In its glorification of "the American spirit of voluntary service, of cooperation, of private and community initiative," the Reagan administration consistently omits references to improvements in the quality of life that have accompanied federal social programs. The claim that government has merely displaced private charity is strongly refuted by qualitative assessments of the impact of public expenditures. Federal support has improved the quality of care for children, the elderly, and other dependents, supplementing the continuing efforts of families and purchasing a greater degree of privacy and autonomy for many adults who prefer to live independently and maintain separate households.[45] While the nostalgic image of home and community care is appealing, in fact it too frequently involved inadequate health care, degrading living conditions, and wide disparities in the availability of support across families, communities, and geographic regions.

Federal assistance to those in need has filled the gaps that always exist between uncoordinated private initiatives, ensuring broad availability of essential services and placing an uneven income floor beneath the poor while also raising standards for provision of such aid. The federal government has played a similar role in complementing the efforts of state and local governments to meet community needs. In most cases where federal aid has been reduced or withdrawn, community leaders and agencies have found it impossible to maintain existing levels of services. Private and public social welfare efforts at the local level, far from being crowded out by federal intervention, have been shored up in diverse and useful ways.

THE ASSAULT ON LOCAL CONTROL

The final refuge of opponents to federal welfare efforts often lies in rigid and outmoded concepts of federalism. In the classic conservative view virtually all responsibilities for social welfare should rest with state and local governments, while the role of the federal government should be limited to selected areas such as national defense and interstate commerce. The argument is that state and local governments, being closer to the people, are better able to assess community needs and to distinguish between the undeserving poor and the truly needy. The fear of federal intrusion and preference for local governance has deep historical roots, reflected in the structure of the Constitution and recurring conflicts over states' rights throughout American history. Local provision of aid to the poor in particular has long-established precedents, dominating welfare laws for more than three centuries from the passage of the English poor laws to the inauguration of the New Deal.

Despite vast social and economic changes conservatives repeatedly invoke this legacy of state and local control in arguing that federal social welfare efforts are counterproductive. "On balance," Martin Anderson wrote, "the closer the level of government is to the people, the more efficient and effective our social welfare programs are apt to be."[46] Similarly, Roger Freeman asserted:

Decisions on whether parents should be required to work—or be partially or wholly exempted because of personal impairment—require individual judgment in each case which can be properly exercised only under local control because no nationally uniform system can do justice to the infinite variety of types of need, individual problems and potentials.[47]

The images evoked in these arguments are of small, closely knit communities uniting together to take care of their problems and residents. Many social needs presumably will be met through private initiatives, but what tasks remain fall to the democratic mechanisms of local government.

Although the appropriate balance of federal, state, and local powers has been debated under every administration, President Reagan has made the issue an integral part of his attack on federal social welfare programs with his proposals for a new federalism:

> [The] massive Federal grantmaking system has distorted State and local decisions and usurped State and local functions . . . . I propose that over the coming years we clean up this mess. I am proposing a major effort to restore American federalism.[48]

> In a single stroke, we will be accomplishing a realignment that will end cumbersome administration and spiraling costs at the Federal level while we insure these programs will be more responsive to both the people they are meant to help and the people who pay for them.[49]

Taking the principle of subsidiarity—namely, that federal government should not undertake functions that can be performed by a lower level of government—to the extreme, Reagan implies that only state and local authorities are competent to identify social needs and to distinguish the deserving poor from the malingerers. Federal intervention is equated with intrusion and waste.

The attempt to decentralize program administration in federal social welfare initiatives can be an appropriate response to regional diversity and centralized bureaucratic inefficiency. However, the Reagan administration has shown little willingness to engage in a thoughtful and objective sorting of federal, state, and local responsibilities. Despite a broad consensus that income maintenance should be financed at the federal level in a national battle against poverty, President Reagan has sought to transfer AFDC and other income transfer programs serving able-bodied recipients into the states' domain. In return the administration has proposed federalization of Medicaid, an entitlement program in which waste, fraud, and abuse have been reduced as a result of state cost control and enforcement efforts. If a reevaluation of federalism is to be constructive it must begin with a more realistic appraisal of the resources and capabilities present at each level of government and the nature of the problems that are being attacked.

The administration has defended its proposals to decentralize welfare by citing its belief that "income redistribution is not a compelling justification in the 1980s for Federal taxing and spending programs."[50] The unspoken intent of Reagan's new federalism proposals is also to strengthen the links between income transfers and low-wage labor markets. Elimination of a federal role in income maintenance for the able-bodied poor would enhance the ability of state and local officials to maintain benefit levels below prevailing wage rates, thereby ensuring the availability of low-wage labor in local labor markets. Critics of federal intervention promote these interests when they euphemistically declare that "communities should be able to decide on the standards at which they wish to support their needy members."[51]

As in the case of voluntarism, conservatives seek to obscure the reasons why federal social welfare programs have grown in recent decades. Contrary to the idealized notion of community responsibility, state and local governments consistently failed to marshal the will and the resources to alleviate poverty and expand economic opportunity for the most disadvantaged prior to federal intervention. By definition the poorest states and localities faced the most severe problems while having the least capacity to redress them. Competition among states also discourages individual states from taking a lead in expanding outlays for welfare programs while contiguous states hold back. The federal government, with its broader and more equitable financing structures and revenue base, is far more able to support income maintenance and large-scale human resource programs. Past experience strongly suggests that if the call to return social welfare responsibilities to state and local governments were heeded the result would not be more responsive aid but simply less aid to those in need.

A recent study of the effects of federal spending cuts on state and local governments demonstrated that such concern is well justified. Close examination of the nature and impact of changes in fourteen states and forty local governments during 1982 revealed that only about one-fourth of all cuts in federal funding for employment and job training, compensatory education, health and social services, and entitlement grants were replaced by states and localities. In some cases the effects of the cuts were delayed by utilizing carryover federal grant funds, thus offsetting the immediate cuts and delaying their ultimate impact. However, as tighter eligibility requirements trimmed AFDC and food stamp rolls, several states even enjoyed net savings. The cuts in entitlement programs were the least likely to be replaced, leaving the working poor who were on the margin of income eligibility for means-tested programs most affected by reductions in federal aid.[52]

Some critics of federal social welfare programs defend this result, citing as justification the charges of waste and counterproductivity already discussed. Others still contend that if unmet needs were real and pressing, state and local governments would step in to fill current federal roles, refusing to acknowledge the barriers to broad political representation which decentralization creates. By placing decisionmaking authority in state houses and city or town halls, opponents of antipoverty efforts would succeed in fragmenting the constituencies that support aid to the needy, reducing the visibility of social problems and restricting the policy options available to public officials to adopt potential remedies.[53] This political strategy constitutes an important hidden agenda in the federalism debate and renders the allegedly greater responsiveness of state and local governments largely irrelevant to prospects for aid to the poor under a decentralized system. Many state and local officials would strive to meet the most pressing social needs in their jurisdictions if federal support were withdrawn, but the means at their disposal would normally be very limited.

This argument does not negate the fact that in some realms decentralized decisionmaking and program administration is crucial to the effectiveness of government efforts. However, many pervasive social ills are national in scope and cannot be addressed efficiently or effectively at the local level. Even in traditionally local areas of responsibility, such as education, a federal role is necessary to ensure the availability of resources in impoverished regions, to reduce the duplication of efforts that occurs when separate jurisdictions reinvent the wheel, and to facilitate improvements in knowledge and practice pertaining to complex social problems. These federal activities have not hampered related state, local, or private initiatives in the past. Rather, federal intervention has increased the total resources devoted to alleviation of the nation's social problems and strengthened the safety net that protects the well-being of all Americans.

NOTES

1. George Gilder, *Wealth and Poverty* (New York: Basic Books, 1981), p. 12.
2. Lawrence M. Mead, "Social Programs and Social Obligations," *Public Interest*, Fall 1982, pp. 18–19.
3. George Gilder, "Why I Am Not A Neo-Conservative," *National Review*, March 5, 1982, p. 219; George Gilder, *Wealth and Poverty*, p. 92.
4. Roger A. Freeman, *The Wayward Welfare State* (Stanford, Cal.: Hoover Institution Press, 1981), pp. 64–65.
5. Ronald Reagan, *The Creative Society* (New York: The Devin-Adair Co., 1968), p. 4.

6. Clifford Orwin, "Welfare and the New Dignity," *Public Interest,* Spring 1983, pp. 87–88.
7. Milton and Rose Friedman, *Free to Choose* (New York: Harcourt Brace Jovanovich, 1980), pp. 109–110, 118.
8. George Gilder, "Family, Faith, and Economic Progress," *National Review,* April 15, 1983, p. 429.
9. Ronald Reagan, December 3, 1983.
10. Bureau of the Census, *Money Income and Poverty Status of Families and Persons in the United States,* 1982, Series P-60, No. 140, p. 4.
11. "A Dream Deferred: The Economic Status of Black Americans" (Washington, D.C.: Center for the Study of Social Policy, July 1983), p. 4.
12. George Gilder, *Wealth and Poverty,* pp. 114–15.
13. Ibid., p. 12.
14. Heather Ross and Isabel Sawhill, *Time of Transition: The Growth of Families Headed By Women* (Washington, D.C.: The Urban Institute, 1976), pp. 10, 118.
15. Robert Lerman, "The Family, Poverty, and Welfare Programs: An Introductory Essay on Problems of Analysis and Policy," in U.S. Congress, Joint Economic Committee, *Studies in Public Welfare* (Washington, D.C.: U.S. Government Printing Office, 1974), pp. 18–19.
16. Lyle P. Groeneveld, Nancy Brandon Tuma, and Michael T. Hannan, "The Effects of Negative Income Tax Programs on Marital Dissolution," *Journal of Human Resources,* Fall 1980, pp. 654–74.
17. Marjorie Honig, "The Impact of Welfare Payment Levels on Family Stability," in U.S. Congress, Joint Economic Committee, *Studies in Public Welfare,* pp. 37–53.
18. Quoted in Judith Cummings, "Breakup of Black Family Imperils Gains of Decades," *New York Times,* November 20, 1983, p. 56.
19. *America's New Beginning: A Program for Economic Recovery* (Washington, D.C.: Executive Office of the President, February 18, 1981), p. 21.
20. Michael Novak, "The Moral Case for Reaganomics," *National Review,* May 29, 1981, p. 614.
21. *Economic Report of the President, 1982* (Washington, D.C.: U.S. Government Printing Office, February 1982), p. 92.
22. *Economic Report of the President, 1983* (Washington, D.C.: U.S. Government Printing Office, February 1983), p. 4.
23. Ibid., pp. 39–41.
24. Ronald Reagan, October 4, 1982.
25. Ronald Reagan, September 28, 1982.
26. Ronald Reagan, October 4, 1982.

27. Mark T. Lilla, "The Two Cultures of Political Economy," *Public Interest*, Winter 1981, p. 111.

28. Ben Wattenberg, "Why I Am Not a Neo-Conservative," *National Review*, March 5, 1982, p. 221.

29. Alan S. Blinder, *The Truce in the War on Poverty: Where Do We Go from Here?* (Washington, D.C.: National Policy Exchange, 1982), pp. 10–14.

30. Martin N. Bailey and James Tobin, "Inflation Consequences of Job Creation," in John L. Palmer, ed., *Creating Jobs* (Washington, D.C.: The Brookings Institution, 1978), p. 52.

31. Ronald Reagan, February 20, 1984.

32. Sar A. Levitan and Richard Belous, *More Than Subsistence: Minimum Wages for the Working Poor* (Baltimore, Md.: Johns Hopkins University Press, 1979), pp. 149–64.

33. Ronald Reagan, September 9, 1982.

34. Ronald Reagan, October 4, 1982.

35. Ronald Reagan, September 24, 1981.

36. Lester M. Salamon and Alan J. Abramson, "The Nonprofit Sector," in John L. Palmer and Isabel V. Sawhill, eds., *The Reagan Experiment* (Washington, D.C.: The Urban Institute, 1982), pp. 222–24.

37. Robert A. Nisbet, *Community and Power*, 2nd ed. (New York: Oxford University Press, 1962), p. 98.

38. George Gilder, *Wealth and Poverty*, p. 95.

39. Peter L. Berger and Richard John Neuhaus, *To Empower People: The Role of Mediating Structures in Public Policy* (Washington, D.C.: American Enterprise Institute, 1977), p. 35.

40. Martin Anderson, *Welfare* (Stanford, Cal.: Hoover Institution Press, 1978), p. 166.

41. Susan Rose-Ackerman, "Do Government Grants to Charity Reduce Private Donations?" in Michelle J. White, ed., *Nonprofit Firms in a Three Sector Economy*, COUPE Papers in Public Economics (1982), pp. 95–114.

42. Lester M. Salamon and Alan J. Abramson, "The Nonprofit Sector," in Palmer and Sawhill, *The Reagan Experiment*, pp. 219–42.

43. Lester M. Salamon and Michael F. Gutowski, "Serving Community Needs" (Washington, D.C.: The Urban Institute, 1983).

44. Carol L. Jusenius, "The Economics of Volunteerism: A Review," National Commission for Employment Policy, April 1983 (Unpublished); Paul L. Menchik and Burton A. Weisbrod, "Government Crowding Out and Contributions of Time—Or Why Do People Work For Free," December 1982 (Unpublished).

45. Mary Jo Bane, "Is the Welfare State Replacing the Family?" *Public Interest*, Winter 1983, pp. 97–100.

46. Martin Anderson, *Welfare*, p. 166.

47. Roger A. Freeman, *The Wayward Welfare State*, p. 27.

48. *Budget of the United States Government, 1983* (Washington, D.C.: U.S. Government Printing Office, 1983), p. M22.

49. Ronald Reagan, January 26, 1982.

50. *Economic Report of the President, 1982* (Washington, D.C.: U.S. Government Printing Office, February 1982), p. 92.

51. Roger A. Freeman, *The Wayward Welfare State*, p. 27.

52. Richard P. Nathan and Fred C. Doolittle, *The Consequences of Cuts: The Effects of the Reagan Domestic Program on State and Local Governments* (Princeton, N.J.: Princeton Urban and Regional Research Center, Princeton University, 1983), pp. 5–8, 23–66.

53. Frances Fox Piven and Richard A. Cloward, *The New Class War* (New York: Pantheon, 1982), pp. 129–32.

4

Nothing to Be Done

*[A] man whose labor and self-denial may be
diverted from his maintenance to that of some
other man is not a free man, and approaches
more or less toward the position of a slave....
We shall find that every effort to realize
equality necessitates a sacrifice of liberty.*[1]

—*William Graham Sumner*

Convinced that the poor are responsible for their poverty and
that government aid exacerbates their plight, conservatives
arrive at the inevitable conclusion that poverty is an unavoidable natural state of affairs. Although true believers in
laissez faire anticipate that economic growth will somewhat
alleviate poverty, they accept the notion that some individuals
must fail even in the most affluent society. The penalties of
failure cannot be softened, they contend, because government
intervention to alter market outcomes would diminish the
rewards for achievement and undermine the motivation and
moral character of those it sought to help. Further, conservatives view inequality as inherent in a system that distributes
income on the basis of talent, effort, luck, and merit. About the
resulting deprivation, however unfortunate, there presumably
is nothing to be done.

The determination of conservatives to place the problem
of poverty outside the government's scope of proper responsibilities is revealed most clearly in their polarization of
competing societal values. Arguing that every attempt to aid

the poor is a threat to liberty and a step toward ruthless egalitarianism, conservative ideologues portray freedom as an absolute good that can never be compromised or balanced against other ideals and aspirations. They similarly construe every program that redistributes income as leading irreversibly toward a system that assures equality of result without regard to individual effort or merit. By framing the debate in the context of polar extremes, opponents of federal intervention seek to cast aid to the poor as fundamentally at odds with basic societal values. Lost is the notion of a balance between competing values—one that preserves individual freedoms in the framework of a compassionate welfare state in order to give those freedoms meaning for all its members.

Opponents of federal intervention also justify inaction and resignation amid the persistent failures of free markets by invoking a set of contradictory arguments. They claim that the current combination of in-kind benefits and cash assistance to the poor has eliminated the problem of inadequate income in America and that poverty remains largely a figment of the liberal imagination. Picking up on the notion that the nation's natural rate of unemployment has risen due to structural changes in the economy, laissez faire adherents also imply, paradoxically as it may appear, that forced idleness and related deprivations are normal. Disregarding their internal inconsistency, diverse adherents claim that these eclectic arguments reinforce the theme that the nation has done all it can to combat poverty and inequality of opportunity.

Beneath the rigid polarization of competing ideals and the wide-ranging rationalizations for public inaction, conservative views on poverty and inequality arise out of fundamental value judgments. Adverse to change, they are willing to condone known economic problems and social ills rather than risk the uncertain consequences of federal intervention, and they justify this choice by resorting to a presumably moral claim that we are not our brother's keeper. Thus, the premises of conservative ideology are rooted more in normative judgments than in the nation's experience or empirical evidence and lead to negativism concerning prospects for helping the poor and expanding opportunities for them. A belief in collective responsibility for the deprivation of the least fortunate in American society leads to a very different and compelling view.

THE THREAT TO FREEDOM

Since colonial times political and economic freedoms have been perceived as closely intertwined in the United States. The first settlers, along with generations of immigrants to follow, came to these shores to escape the political or religious oppression and economic restraints of authoritarian governments. Because property rights conferred political rights, strong safeguards were established to prevent the usurpation of private property by government. As America evolved from an agrarian to an advanced and predominant industrial society, the nation's democratic institutions developed more fully and the link between political and economic freedoms became less clear. Nonetheless, the rigid notion that every step toward expanded opportunity places liberty in jeopardy persists, enjoying renewed popularity in the 1980s.

Vigorous assertions of the importance of economic freedom and the dangers of federal intervention emerged in the 1940s in response to the expanding role of government under the New Deal. In his famous work, *The Road to Serfdom,* Friedrich Hayek argued that government bureaucracies by their nature shift decisionmaking away from democratic processes and toward totalitarian or dictatorial control.[2] Similarly, Ludwig von Mises warned of the tendency of government officials to seek ever-larger and more powerful roles and institutions in which to operate.[3] Milton Friedman has reiterated this claim, asserting that government "restrictions on economic freedom inevitably affect freedom in general."[4] Threatened by proposals for greater economic planning, opponents of federal intervention have claimed that bureaucracies administering the welfare programs would escape democratic controls and secure a frightening autonomy. Conservatives quickly dismiss the potential for effective legislative or popular oversight of government initiatives; thus, they perceive the preservation of economic freedoms as indispensable to the protection of political freedom.

As in other areas of conservative ideology, the Reagan administration has presented a remarkably frank defense of the presumed relationship between political and economic freedoms. The 1982 *Economic Report of the President*, calling the link between these freedoms "important" and the evidence to support it "striking," offered the following syllogism:

> All nations which have broad-based representative government and civil liberties have most of their economic activity organized by the market.
>
> Economic conditions in market economies are generally superior to those in nations (with a comparable culture and a comparable resource base) in which the government has the dominant economic role.
>
> No nation in which the government has the dominant economic role (as measured by the proportion of gross national product originating in the government sector) has maintained broad political freedom; economic conditions in such countries are generally inferior to those in comparable nations with a predominantly market economy.[5]

Curiously, the same report notes that the economic role of government in the nations that guarantee their citizens both political and economic freedoms differs widely, without jeopardizing the former. Yet this acknowledgment somehow fails to diminish the Reagan administration's fervor in concluding that an increase in economic freedom will "provide greater assurance of our political freedom."[6]

The simplistic causal relationship implied by the administration—that restrictions on economic freedom necessarily bring curtailment of political freedom—has been described explicitly by former Treasury secretary William E. Simon. Using the Soviet Union as his model of government intervention in the economy, he attempted to demonstrate that the unfortunate consequences of the modern welfare state force us to choose between polar extremes. The Soviet economic controls being oppressive and counterproductive, Simon concluded that the United States must avoid restrictions on free market activities at all costs: "A nation that decreases its economic freedom *must* be less politically free. And because freedom is a precondition for economic creativity and wealth, that nation *must* grow poorer. It follows as night follows day. *If* one understands the polar systems.'" In this view, economic freedoms cannot be constrained without significant losses in political freedom and without declines in economic growth. Simon summarily rejects the idea that a middle ground could provide the optimum balance of competing societal values.

Granted that sharp restrictions on economic choice threaten political freedoms, conservative analysts fail to demonstrate that this crude relationship is relevant to the subtler degrees of economic regulation and income redistribution at issue in modern America. The scope of government intervention in the economy varies widely in France, Sweden, Japan, and the United States, and yet the dominance of political freedom in these nations cannot be seriously questioned. Opponents of federal social welfare initiatives are fond of portraying current programs or any proposed expansion of redistributive measures as an imminent threat to political liberties. In reality, federal efforts to expand the welfare system, including the most ambitious proposals that have received serious congressional consideration during the past two decades, have fallen well within the range of economic constraints already found to be consistent with political freedom in Western European nations.

Conservatives recognize no circumstances in which members of a prosperous and free society might choose to share their acquisitions in pursuit of greater economic security and social justice. Relying on the experience of an earlier, less affluent era, they associate government regulations of guild and colonial vintage with tyranny and view current intervention as inimical to the spirit of entrepreneurship. They perceive, accordingly, the combination of democratic institutions and free markets as the only alternative to this authoritarianism. William Graham Sumner explicitly described the incompatibility of freedom and aid to the poor:

> If any one thinks that there are or ought to be somewhere in society guarantees that no man shall suffer hardship, let him understand that there can be no such guarantees, unless other men give them—that is, unless we go back to slavery, and make one man's effort conduce to another man's welfare.[8]

Even if modern social welfare programs were intended to provide a *guarantee* against hardship—a noble goal far beyond the more immediate objectives of current policies—the required redistribution of income would not constitute a burden so onerous as to be labeled "slavery." Yet, by defining liberty as the total absence of government restrictions or claims on personal resources, conservatives reject even modest steps to reduce hardship through the expansion of opportunity and redistribution of income.

Centrally planned economies instituted by authoritarian governments of course represent the antithesis of freedom. However, the prudent reallocation of economic resources to serve democratically designed and clearly defined goals may have opposite and desired results. With rising affluence it has become conceivable that a free electorate would voluntarily surrender some portion of its economic freedom. As but one example, a payroll tax that "robs" individuals of part of their income provides a guaranteed income to the retired generation while also expanding their options to continue working during their old age or to be relieved from the burdens of the workplace during their declining years. Devotees of laissez faire do not acknowledge this choice as rational but fail to explain how political freedoms were weakened by such restrictions on economic activity.

Opponents of federal intervention ignore the voluntary acceptance of economic restraints in part because they question the legitimacy of public decisionmaking in representative democracies. With a highly individualistic concept of freedom, any form of collective action, even when initiated and ratified through democratic processes, is equated with force and tyranny. As one observer described the conservative's definition of freedom,

> The market offers freedom: if you like Ultra-Glop toothpaste, no one can force you to buy Presto-Goo instead. Government, in contrast, means coercion: if you want your taxes spent on street repairs but a majority of your neighbors are more concerned about fire protection, your dollars are enslaved and shipped off to fill the coffers of the fire department against your will.... Buying and selling are freedom; voting and planning are slavery.[9]

The irony is that, by denying the legitimacy of government decisionmaking, right-wing ideologues denigrate the very political freedoms they purport to defend. Rather than viewing freedom as the opportunity to participate in public decisions, conservatives laud an anarchic independence that makes a mockery of political participation and collective action through democratic means.

Conservative endorsements of unrestrained freedom to pursue individual self-interest may well be self-defeating in a modern era. As Robert Reich has stressed, a philosophy that relies upon the motivational force of greed and fear, allowing no substantial tempering of the extremes of affluence and deprivation, necessarily undermines the potential for cooperation in advanced societies:

> A society that offers both the prospect of substantial wealth and the threat of severe poverty surely will inspire great feats of personal daring, dazzling entrepreneurialism, and cutthroat ambition. But

just as surely it may reduce the capacity of its members to work together toward a common end. The conservative promise of prosperity is an ideology suited to a frontier economy in which risk-taking is apt to be more socially productive than cooperation, but it is hardly appropriate to an advanced industrial economy in which collaboration is critical.[10]

The complex social and economic problems of the 1980s cannot be addressed unless American society has the capacity to decide collectively what needs to be done and to marshal the resources to do it. By casting government action as a threat to liberty, conservatives impede the nation's progress.

OPPORTUNITY VERSUS EQUALITY OF RESULT

The confusion and misrepresentations of conservatives are nowhere more evident than in the debate between equality of opportunity and equality of result in the modern welfare state. Accepting the goal of equality of opportunity, the serious and legitimate debate in mainstream American politics turns on the question of the appropriate steps that should be taken to promote and ensure this equality and the speed with which it is to be attained. At a minimum, equality of opportunity requires the protection of basic civil rights, the elimination of discriminatory practices in the economy, and universal access to public services. Yet equal opportunity may remain elusive for segments of society unless the effects of past and present discrimination are offset through more active government interventions. For this reason numerous policy initiatives over the past two decades have attempted to meet basic human needs and to provide remedial or compensatory aid through employment, training, and affirmative action programs as a means of opening both entry-level jobs and opportunities for advancement.

Critics of the welfare system consistently attempt to portray federal interventions and regulations as insatiable drives toward radical income redistribution. Although the subject of frequent philosophical debate, a strict egalitarian goal has never been the intent of American public policy, nor has it been embraced by major political leaders or parties in the United States. Nonetheless, opponents of federal intervention insist that the modern welfare state pushes society inevitably toward an unattainable equality of result and that social welfare programs are designed to serve that illusory goal. The perceived link between egalitarianism and the expansion of government responsibilities has become a central theme in modern conservative thought, buttressing the conclusion that poverty is inevitable in a free and equitable society.

The preoccupation of conservatives with egalitarian thought is pervasive and frequently indistinguishable from libertarian doctrine. They have claimed that "liberalism pushes with increasing aggressiveness for equality," abandoning "America's unique meritocratic tradition that for generations has rewarded achievement and fostered social mobility."[11] Simon identifies striving for equal opportunity with "equality of outcome," which he insists requires that everyone "finish the race at the same time .... in clear conflict with liberty."[12] The United States, according to the Friedmans, has become "purely and simply a redistributionist state, endlessly shaking down Peter to pay Paul," a nation in which "leveling" is the dominant goal.[13]

By linking social welfare programs and egalitarianism, conservative ideologues portray federal intervention as antithetical to meritocratic norms. They attempt to fan public fears of injustice at every turn, tying federal social welfare efforts to egalitarian ideals which

> wrest the rewards away from those who have earned them and give them to those who have not .... The more one achieves, the more one is punished; the less one achieves, the more one is rewarded. Egalitarianism is a morbid assault on both ability and justice. Its goal is not to enhance individual achievement; it is to *level* all men.[14]

These assaults on federal intervention make no mention of the role of the state in shaping earning opportunities in the marketplace nor of the large measures of luck that combine with effort and talent to determine personal income.

A policy the goal of which is to achieve equality of result would be subject to challenge on both moral and pragmatic grounds. Henry Hazlitt has articulated the moral objection to such a policy:

> If you claim a 'right' to an income sufficient to live in dignity, whether you are willing to work or not, what you are really claiming is a right to part of somebody else's earned income. What you are asserting is that this other person has a duty to earn more than he needs or wants to live on, so that the surplus may be seized from him and turned over to you to live on. This is an absolutely immoral proposition.[15]

In addition to the perceived inequity of these transfers conservatives lament the "assault on earned dignity" which detaches achievement from deserts, robbing those with ability and motivation of the pride and distinction that would otherwise accompany their efforts.[16] Redistributive policies, therefore, are judged to be both wrong and counterproductive.

Conservatives create a classic straw man when they attempt to cast liberal social welfare policies as a denial of differences in achievement or a threat to meritocratic rewards. Federal social welfare programs since the early 1960s have sought to expand opportunity and minimize the hardships of the unfettered market through modest reductions in income inequality, never seeking or endorsing the unattainable equality of result. Federal intervention during this period has increased because most Americans distinguish between government intervention to expand economic opportunity or to meet basic needs and broader attempts to redistribute income.

Although a majority of Americans profess a dislike for big government in the abstract, they continue to support a major federal role in seeing that the poor are cared for, that no one goes hungry, and that every person achieves a minimum standard of living. A 1981 Harris Survey showed Americans favoring federal responsibility in these areas by 72 to 26 percent. More recent polls continue to provide evidence of support for federal employment, training, health care, and education programs, despite Reagan administration assaults on these programs.[17]

There are limits beyond which the tax burden required to support social programs might stifle achievement and initiative by dramatically reducing rewards for individual effort. The 1981 personal income tax cuts were rooted in the claim of supply-side economics that progressive federal tax and transfer policies had already reached this counterproductive stage and that reductions in marginal tax rates would increase economic growth as well as government revenues. The anticipated boom in economic activity and subsequent tax revenues has not materialized, creating the ominous prospect of huge and lasting federal deficits which could impair future economic growth. The results of the Reagan experiment certainly do not suggest that social programs have deprived the affluent of the fruits of achievement in order to open opportunities for the less fortunate.

If the welfare state stifles achievement and deprives individuals of the fruits of their labor, it does so among the working poor rather than the affluent. The Reagan administration's social welfare policies have been properly criticized because they presume that the rich can be enticed to work harder with a carrot while the poor require a stick. The prohibitively high marginal tax rates that President Reagan has imposed on welfare recipients foreclose numerous opportunities for advancement through individual effort. In the process conservatives have come far closer to insisting on equality of result than any prior federal social welfare initiatives, foreclosing opportunities of many impoverished Americans to raise their meager incomes regardless of how hard they work.

POVERTY—A FIGMENT OF IMAGINATION?

Beyond their visions of tyranny and egalitarianism, conservatives invoke a wide range of arguments to bolster their claim that poverty is inevitable. George Gilder has concluded that "there will be poverty in America for centuries to come."[18] President Reagan has long associated the persistence of poverty with "the inadequacy of human nature" and assailed proposed federal remedies as "untried theory packaged as Utopia."[19] His administration has stressed the superiority of free markets over the imperfections of government interventions in resolving conflicts, echoing assertions made by Governor Reagan in the 1960s that "big government . . . is incompetent to deliver many of its promises."[20] These claims ignore the potential for refining federal interventions and thereby making incremental gains in the fight against poverty. Deprivation and hardship are posed as facts that the nation must accept, unfortunate but unavoidable realities about the way the world works.

Conservatives assuage their conscience by insisting that the poverty problem is not as bad as it seems. Repeating a constant refrain, Simon contended that poverty is in part an invention of "new class" liberals whose livelihood depends upon an ever-growing population served by social programs.[21] A similar questioning of motives and integrity is reflected in charges that proponents of aid to the poor are guided by envy of the rich rather than by objectivity and compassion. President Reagan has suggested repeatedly that poverty and welfare dependency is perpetuated by bureaucrats and program administrators who enhance their own wealth and importance at the expense of the truly productive.[22] It is as though census data showing that poverty has been on the rise since 1978 and that some 34 million Americans live in poverty are not adequate and legitimate cause for concern.

Reports of growing hunger are similarly dismissed. Despite a large increase in the number of privately organized and operated food assistance outlets and an increase in the number of people who seek help from them, the Reagan administration proposed sharp reductions in food assistance in the midst of a deep recession. President Reagan's Task Force on Food Assistance, noting that hunger does persist, still claimed that administration-proposed cutbacks were not responsible, and administration officials have accused those standing in soup lines of ripping off food giveaway programs while their cupboards remained full. The task force's primary remedy—additional business tax breaks for donations combined with tighter eligibility requirements for food aid recipients—certainly belies the administration's professed "deep concern" for the hunger problem.

In recent years opponents of government intervention have attempted to discredit or explain away official statistical measures of unemployment and poverty. Emphasizing the value of federally subsidized food stamps, housing, medical care, and other in-kind benefits not considered in government data, some critics of the welfare system have declared victory in the war on poverty, precluding the need for further efforts.[23] Yet the Census Bureau estimates of the value of in-kind assistance to the poor suggest that poverty certainly has not disappeared from our midst. Depending upon the methodology used in making estimates, the number of poor in the United States in 1982 is reduced by between 9 and 33 percent from official levels when in-kind transfers are counted as income. However, the same study found that poverty increased by 47 percent (from 6.8 to 10 percent) between 1979 and 1982 even after the inclusion of noncash benefits—a rate well above the official 28 percent increase in poverty when cash income alone is considered. As a result of the 10.4 percent decline in the average market value of noncash benefits between 1979 and 1982, these benefits were significantly less effective in reducing poverty in 1982 than three years earlier.[24]

The hypocrisy of conservatives who claim the war on poverty has been won and subsequently endorse cuts in federal social welfare programs is blatant. In the absence of any federal aid to the poor, 23 percent of all Americans would have lived in poverty in 1981, compared to the official rate of 14 percent.[25] For nearly one in ten Americans federal social welfare programs provided the added income necessary to lift their households out of poverty. Federal in-kind benefits brought relief from deprivation for additional millions with cash incomes below the poverty line. The refinement of official poverty statistics provides further evidence that federal intervention has succeeded in alleviating hardship and offers no basis for reducing federal social welfare expenditures without reversing past gains.

The very effectiveness of federal welfare programs has also encouraged opponents of federal intervention to explain away rising unemployment rates as more tolerable and more natural than in prior eras. In defense of sharp increases in joblessness under the Reagan economic program, his administration argued that the lowest unemployment rate compatible with stable prices has risen substantially during the past two decades, the result of demographic changes as well as the "behavioral and reporting effects" of social programs on the measured unemployment rate.[26] President Reagan has advanced the parallel claim that the "normal unemployment rate—which is based on . . . the people who are between jobs or have quit a job to try for another one, this sort of thing— may, instead of being the 4 percent that we used to talk about, it may be 6 or 6½ percent."[27] The thrust of these claims is to suggest that higher rates of unemployment are not "a reflection of a bad economy," but rather represent natural changes in the labor market that offer no cause for alarm.

The notion that frictional unemployment necessarily leaves at least 7 million Americans without work is grossly misleading. While research findings suggest that the availability of unemployment insurance and other social welfare benefits is responsible for a small rise in the underlying unemployment rate, joblessness can be plausibly reduced to below 5 percent if appropriate action is taken to remove obstacles to employment. Joblessness far above this level cannot be attributed to voluntary job changes and temporary job search and can be assumed to arise from causes that can be ameliorated through government action. Furthermore, even if one accepted the Reagan administration's view of the normal or natural rate of unemployment, this rationalization offers no excuse for its refusal to respond to record joblessness that existed in 1982 and continued at a high level during the succeeding year.

The perversity of conservative challenges to official unemployment statistics again lies in their desire to reduce or eliminate the very social welfare benefits that they contend make high unemployment rates tolerable. Asserting that efforts to eliminate curable poverty have been successful, advocates of retrenchment justify their position as though the victory they imagine could be permanent. The fact is, however, that the bulk of progress in alleviating deprivation in modern America has come through federal income transfer programs, and the Reagan administration's budget cuts have already demonstrated that reductions in this aid lead to increases in poverty. If conservatives truly believed that the plight of the poor has improved, they would be obliged to support the programs that have facilitated such gains. Few have proved so consistent in their approach to poverty and social justice in the United States.

INDIVIDUAL CHOICE AND SOCIAL CHANGE

Social change necessarily challenges established values and institutions. Conservatives find it tempting to blame government programs for the evolutionary processes that they find threatening, even when the link between federal efforts and social change cannot be established. Anticipating disastrous consequences from contemporary trends, they prefer the certainty that government will not accelerate change to any benefits that federal intervention might bring.

In so doing conservatives place themselves in opposition to not only government responsibility for social welfare but also the legitimacy of personal choice in a free and open society.

The social changes that conservatives lament are the products of diverse individual decisions made by millions of Americans. Whether to end a marriage, accept income transfers, or relinquish religious and cultural ties are difficult and painful personal choices seldom taken lightly. In some instances government intervention has established perverse incentives, forcing families to dissolve in order to subsist or rendering welfare more attractive than work. However, in most cases conservatives simply dislike the individual value judgments reflected in patterns of social change. By seeking to preserve the status quo they are forced to deny the sanctity of personal choice which they presumably revere.

It is important to recognize that the detrimental impact of social change is not as evident as conservatives would have us believe. Does the moral degradation of welfare dependency impose more hardship than material deprivation? Were the strained marriages of yesterday necessarily better than the pain and turmoil of today's divorces? Did the closely knit organic communities of the past offer a more hospitable environment for the poor than the current welfare system? In each case conservatives glorify old patterns and practices while ignoring the compensating advantages of social change. A more objective view would document gains as well as losses, citing the freedoms and benefits of emerging institutional arrangements while remaining cognizant of the price that has been paid for them.

Conservatives' resistance to the cumulative results of personal choice is closely related to their portrayal of poverty as a moral problem. Despite their laissez faire ideology opponents of government intervention are reluctant to view low-income Americans as capable of rational decisions that promote their well-being. The poor presumably are irresponsible and unable to make prudent judgments or shun immediate gratification for long-term benefit. Hence, the choices made by low-income persons regarding their families, incomes, and future prospects allegedly tend to run counter to both the national interest and their own narrow self-interest. Conservatives believe that unless the decisions of the poor are altered, government aid to them may only accelerate their demise.

The logical conclusion, if one follows this line of reasoning, is an endorsement of paternalism sharply at odds with a commitment to individual freedoms. Indeed, the refusal to accept the legitimacy of the choices the poor make negates traditional conservative views. True to the conservative creed, Reagan administration economists have explicitly rejected a paternalistic approach to the needs of the poor:

> Paternalism occurs when the government is reluctant to let individuals make decisions for themselves and seeks to protect them from the possible bad effects of their own decisions by outlawing certain actions. Paternalism has the effect of disallowing certain preferences or actions. This Administration rejects paternalism as a basis for policy. There is no reason to think that commands from government can do a better job of increasing an individual's economic welfare than the individual can by making choices himself. Moreover, the long-term cost of paternalism may be to destroy an individual's ability to make decisions for himself.[28]

Nonetheless, the administration has challenged the ability of the poor to make crucial decisions regarding their families, dignity, and future well-being, contending that social welfare programs induce low-income Americans to act contrary to their best interests.

One need not cast the poor as incompetent to account for their plight. Evidence of unequal opportunity and barriers to economic advancement in contemporary labor markets provides ample basis for an alternative view of poverty and dependence—one that avoids paternalism and respects the integrity of personal choice. The contradictions of laissez faire advocates strongly suggest that their opposition to federal intervention in aid of the poor is rooted more in their apprehension of social change than in a realistic appraisal of the nature and causes of poverty. Given a different set of value judgments—ones that place social progress and justice before the protection of vested interests—the importance of federal intervention in aid of the poor cannot be denied.

POVERTY AND DEPENDENCY— AN ALTERNATIVE VIEW

A realistic account of work and poverty in the United States should begin with an acknowledgment that the great majority of the poor do not lack work motivation. Although unwillingness to work poses a threat of dependency within a small segment of the welfare population, most impoverished adults face numerous barriers to employment and advancement, including aggregate job deficits, educational deficiencies, geographic isolation, discriminatory employment practices, lack of prior work experience, and a perverse welfare structure that frequently discriminates against the working poor. A large portion of those living in poverty already work, many in full-time jobs, but the low wage rates that prevail in secondary labor markets are inadequate to lift the working poor above the poverty threshold. Because work and poverty are not mutually exclusive, only government policies that combine work and welfare can adequately address the needs of the low-income population.

While the poor in general seem to have as much of a commitment to work as do higher income groups, they are not oblivious to rational calculations regarding the returns of work and the marginal utility of income versus leisure. Without accepting the conservative conclusion that welfare benefits are too generous, one can still share the concern of welfare critics that high marginal tax rates for the poor have the potential for creating a "poverty wall" which "destroys their incentive to work and sentences them to a life of dependency on the government dole."[29] The experience of the past two decades suggests that income transfers can alleviate poverty by placing a floor of minimum benefits beneath the poor, but in the absence of initiatives to tap their work motivation too many of them will find a steady, albeit minimal, source of income preferable to the uncertainties of low-paid work. Welfare policies can avoid the no-win choice between deprivation and dependency only if they are structured to provide rewards for work effort and if they are accompanied by programs to promote work opportunities.

Opponents of government intervention who harp on the motivation of the poor seldom acknowledge that their willingness to work has never been tested in peacetime through the aggressive expansion of employment opportunities. Although Great Society rhetoric placed a strong emphasis on opportunity, transfer payments and in-kind assistance far surpassed expenditures on education, training, employment, community organization, and social service initiatives, leaving the potential for expanded work experience among the poor largely unrealized. This pattern has been repeated in more perverse fashion during the Reagan administration: despite its presumed commitment to opportunity as an alternative to welfare dependency, the administration's opposition to spending for employment, education, and social services has left federal domestic activities increasingly dominated by cash transfer and health-financing programs.[30] Even as social spending has grown steadily, opportunity has taken a back seat to income maintenance.

Given the absence of opportunities and the limited rewards for work when jobs are available, it is perhaps surprising that the poor have not responded to subsistence benefits and high marginal tax rates by dropping out of the labor force in far greater numbers. Research findings suggest that when welfare recipients are faced with benefit reduction rates of less than 100 percent, their work effort is affected only moderately by variations in benefit levels and marginal tax rates.[31] This commitment to work has been exploited by the

Reagan administration, which has reduced the returns from labor for those on AFDC while relying on the strength of the work ethic to stem the shift toward greater dependency and higher long-term welfare costs. A more compassionate and constructive policy would tap the desire and willingness of the poor to work by bolstering job availability, strengthening the education and training opportunities that contribute to upward mobility, and supplementing low wages in secondary labor markets.

The existing welfare system gives partial recognition to the interrelationships between work and welfare, helping many Americans and allowing some flexibility for movement in and out of the labor market. Yet sharp restrictions on aid to the working poor still confine some recipients to dependency and threaten to create a permanent underclass. A public policy that expects low-income Americans to make rational calculations regarding the costs and rewards of work as compared to welfare must ensure that work is more renumerative than welfare. Past federal approaches to combat poverty have fallen far short of this fundamental goal.

To minimize conflicts between work and welfare, federal programs in aid of the poor must recognize the limitations of private labor markets in offering employment opportunities that permit the unemployed and the working poor to escape poverty. The world of opportunity, upward mobility, and adequate wages envisioned by conservatives does not exist for large segments of the low-income population. A commitment to work and self-sufficiency through government initiative would represent a sharp departure from the rhetoric of those who, in Peter Edelman's words, "would engage in further punishment of the millions who lack skills or, having skills, lack the possibility of obtaining employment because there are not enough jobs to go around."[32] Yet this is the task that remains before the nation, for it is the barriers to advancement and self-support in the labor market, not the ministrations of government, that most directly hinder the rise from poverty in modern America.

NOTES

1. William Graham Sumner, *What Social Classes Owe To Each Other* (New York: Harper and Bros., 1883), p. 15.
2. Friedrich A. Hayek, *The Road to Serfdom* (Chicago: University of Chicago Press, 1944).
3. Ludwig von Mises, *Bureaucracy* (New Haven: Yale University Press, 1944).
4. Milton and Rose Friedman, *Free to Choose* (New York: Harcourt Brace Jovanovich, 1980), p. 58.
5. *Economic Report of the President, 1982* (Washington, D.C.: U.S. Government Printing Office, February 1982), p. 27.
6. Ibid., p. 28.
7. William E. Simon, *A Time for Truth* (New York: McGraw-Hill, 1978), p. 32.
8. William Graham Sumner, *What Social Classes Owe To Each Other*, p. 24.
9. Frank Ackerman, *Reaganomics: Rhetoric vs. Reality* (Boston: South End Press, 1982), p. 20.
10. Robert B. Reich, "The Liberal Promise of Prosperity," *New Republic*, February 21, 1981, p. 23.
11. Burton Yale Pine, *Back to Basics* (New York: William Morrow, 1982), p. 22.
12. William E. Simon, *A Time For Truth*, p. 210.
13. Milton and Rose Friedman, *Free to Choose*, p. 119.
14. William E. Simon, *A Time for Truth*, p. 200.
15. Henry Hazlitt, quoted in Chamber of Commerce of the United States, *Proceedings of the National Symposium on Guaranteed Income*, Washington, D.C., December 9, 1966, p. 13.
16. Clifford Orwin, "Welfare and the New Dignity," *Public Interest*, Spring 1983, p. 91.
17. Harris Surveys, March 1981, December 1982, April 1983; Roper Opinion Poll, November 1981; Seymour Martin Lipset and Earl Raab, "The Message of Proposition 13," *Commentary*, September 1978, pp. 44–45.
18. George Gilder, *Wealth and Poverty* (New York: Basic Books, 1981), p. 67.
19. Ronald Reagan, *The Creative Society* (New York: The Devin-Adair Co., 1968), p. 122.
20. *Economic Report of the President, 1982*, p. 27; Ronald Reagan, *The Creative Society*, p. 77.
21. William E. Simon, *A Time For Truth*, p. 210.
22. Ronald Reagan, September 9, 1982.

23. Martin Anderson, *Welfare* (Stanford, Cal.: Hoover Institution Press, 1978), p.15; Charles A. Murray, "The Two Wars Against Poverty: Economic Growth and the Great Society," *Public Interest,* Fall 1982, p. 8.

24. U.S. Bureau of the Census, *Estimates of the Poverty Population Including the Value of Noncash Benefits: 1979–1982,* Technical Paper No. 52 (Washington, D.C.: U.S. Government Printing Office, 1984).

25. Linda E. Demkovich and Joel Havemann, "The Poor and the Near Poor May Be Bearing the Brunt," *National Journal,* October 23, 1982, p. 1796.

26. *Economic Report of the President, 1983* (Washington, D.C.: U.S. Government Printing Office, February 1983), pp. 3738.

27. Ronald Reagan, October 4, 1982.

28. *Economic Report of the President 1982,* p. 42.

29. Martin Anderson, *Welfare,* p. 50.

30. John L. Palmer and Gregory B. Mills, "Budget Policy," in John L. Palmer and Isabel V. Sawhill, eds., *The Reagan Experiment* (Washington, D.C.: The Urban Institute Press, 1982), p. 76.

31. Robert A. Moffit, "The Effect of a Negative Income Tax on Work Effort: A Summary of the Experimental Results," in Paul M. Somers, ed., *Welfare Reform in America: Perspectives and Prospects* (Boston: Kluwer-Nijhoff Publishing, 1982); Sheldon Danziger, Robert Haveman, and Robert Plotnick, "How Income Transfer Programs Affect Work, Savings, and the Income Distribution: A Critical Review," *Journal of Economic Literature,* September 1981, pp. 975–1028.

32. Peter Edelman, "Work and Welfare: An Alternative Perspective on Entitlements," in *Budget and Policy Choices 1983* (Washington, D.C.: Center for National Policy, 1983), p. 54.

5

Programs that Made a Difference

This nation, this people, this generation, has man's first chance to create a Great Society: a society of success without squalor, beauty without barrenness, works of genius without the wretchedness of poverty. We can open the doors of learning. We can open the doors of fruitful labor and rewarding leisure, of open opportunity and close community—not just to the privileged few, but to everyone.[1]

—Lyndon B. Johnson

Social and economic developments in the United States have repeatedly challenged conservative views on the necessary roles of government. Amid the mass joblessness and abject poverty of the 1930s, government acquiescence to sharp savings in the business cycle threatened the stability of the economic system, and unemployment could no longer be viewed as a temporary phenomenon or product of inadequate work motivation. In the postwar period evidence of race discrimination and widespread deprivation brought to national attention by the civil rights movement and related antipoverty efforts further discredited the conservative faith in the strong link between individual merit and market rewards. As research on the nation's social problems has grown more sophisticated, the barriers to advancement and opportunity obscured by laissez faire ideology have grown increasingly evident.

American social welfare policies have changed dramatically over the past five decades in response to these developments. The basic foundations of the modern welfare system which were fought bitterly by conservatives as antithetical to a free society—social security, unemployment compensation, and health care—are now accepted across the political spectrum. Public investments in education, health care, housing, nutrition, and income maintenance have reached levels unforeseen even twenty years ago. Federal aid to the poor approaches a comprehensive, albeit not universal, system providing subsistence income for those in need. Progress in these diverse areas has not been achieved as quickly or easily as many had hoped, but it has been appreciable and undeniable.

The nation's social welfare experience from Roosevelt to Reagan is replete with lessons that refute conservative negativism and provide a framework for the modern welfare state. The basic needs of most Americans for food, clothing, and shelter have been met. The health and longevity of all population groups in the United States have been improved. Opportunities for education, training, and employment have been expanded, particularly for low-income segments of the work force and among poor youth. Discrimination based on race, sex, and age has diminished, and new employment and housing opportunities have been opened to previously excluded members of our society. Notwithstanding popular perceptions of waste and incompetence, federal social welfare programs during the last two generations have achieved striking gains and provide a foundation on which future government strategies in social welfare can be based.

A RECORD OF FEDERAL ACHIEVEMENT

The accomplishments of the welfare system are readily apparent. The Social Security Act of 1935 and subsequent extensions of its coverage and levels of benefits have sharply reduced deprivation among orphans, the disabled and the aged, provided a cushion for those forced into temporary idleness, and extended support to poverty-stricken families with children and to the permanently disabled. The elderly today are less likely to suffer economic hardship than are younger Americans—the result of dramatic expansions in public and private pension benefits—and the great majority are guaranteed adequate health care in their retirement years. Although less true of the deep 1981–82 recession than those preceding it since World War II, the likelihood of jobless Americans slipping into poverty has also been reduced by the enhanced availability of unemployment insurance benefits. Any modern-day Rip Van Winkle who awoke in 1984 surely would be struck by this system of social insurance against the infirmities of old age and the deprivations of forced idleness.

Other achievements of the modern welfare system are more narrowly focused or difficult to quantify and are therefore less broadly recognized. Seeking to bolster opportunity and minimize hardship from cradle to grave, federal social welfare programs have proved effective in expanding access to education and employment while also meeting basic human needs. Moreover, in the early stages of life federal intervention has improved prospects for advancement and future self-sufficiency. The modern welfare system's goals of expanded opportunity and reduced deprivation throughout the life cycle reflect the maturation of a productive and affluent society and offer a continuing agenda for progress toward a greater society.[2]

Infant Mortality and Child Nutrition

Recognizing that large families and unwanted births increase the probability that households will be destitute, the federal government supports family planning services for low-income individuals. By assisting families in avoiding out-of-wedlock births and unplanned pregnancies, federal efforts to promote effective birth control help to prevent households from being driven into poverty by unwanted children while also substantially improving health among the poor. Fertility control lowers maternal and infant mortality rates and reduces the incidence of mental retardation, physical defects, and premature births. In addition, children in smaller families tend to receive better care and support, becoming less likely candidates for a life of poverty than children from large families.[3]

Nutritional deficiencies can widen disparities in opportunity even prior to birth. The federal government has sought to mitigate barriers to advancement at the beginning of the life cycle through a special supplemental food program for women, infants, and children (WIC). Low-income mothers, infants, and children suffering from poor nutrition are eligible to receive food or vouchers that can be exchanged for milk, cereals, juices, and other selected food items. WIC recipients, whose nutritional needs must be certified by a competent professional authority to qualify for benefits, often have incomes well below the poverty line: the annual family income of participants in 1978 was 20 percent below the poverty threshold. Nationally, 2.4 million women received a WIC food package valued at $378 in fiscal year 1983.

Federal provision of balanced diets, nutritional education, and health services to low-income pregnant women, nursing mothers, infants, and children under five years of age have significantly increased the likelihood of normal deliveries and healthy children among poor families. The WIC program has been credited with marked reductions in the incidence of low-birth-weight infants, with resulting savings in hospital costs for extended care estimated at $3 for every $1 spent in the WIC prenatal component.[4] The Massachusetts Department of Public Health has noted a decline in infant mortality; the Center for Disease Control found marked reductions in infants suffering from anemia. These medical developments, a product of federal intervention, are important factors in overall efforts to prevent retarded physical growth, susceptibility to disease, and mental retardation, thereby improving possibilities for future self-sufficiency.

The federal government continues its food assistance efforts for older children through the school lunch, school breakfast, and special milk programs. The largest federal child nutrition effort, the school lunch program, served 23.6 million youngsters in fiscal year 1982 at a total cost of $2.9 billion. In conjunction with the breakfast and special milk programs, these subsidized meals administered by local schools in many cases provide the sole nutritional meal each day that poor and near-poor children receive. While the absence of narrow targeting of benefits in child nutrition programs has drawn criticism from some quarters, relatively broad eligibility requirements have responded to the need for economies of scale in program administration and have contributed to a solid base of political support for child nutrition efforts.

Beyond nutritional assistance preventive medical services for mothers, infants, and children are supported by the federal government through grants to states for maternal and child health and through Medicaid. In 1981, 17 million pregnant women and children were served by the maternal and child health block grant program and Medicaid paid for the health care of more than 10 million poor children. The results of specific federal interventions in preventive health care have been impressive. A Texas study found that the state saved $8 in avoided medical costs for every $1 spent on preventive services, and a North Dakota analysis showed that Medicaid costs for children who received preventive health care dropped by one-third.[5] Preventive services clearly are effective in both improving infant and child health and saving taxpayers' money.

In more general ways federal initiatives have sought to expand the availability of health care in regions heavily populated by low-income Americans and underserved by private medical practitioners. Federal policy has encouraged health care personnel to reside in impoverished rural and urban areas through the provision of medical education scholarships and loan deferments. A targeted approach yielding dramatic results can be found in the record of the Indian Health Service, created to meet the acute health needs of isolated and poverty-stricken native Americans. As a result of this targeted federal effort, Indian life expectancy increased 5.1 years in the two decades following 1950, driven in part by a drop in the infant mortality rate from 61 to 18 deaths per 1,000 live births between 1960 and 1977. Reliance on free markets could not have produced improvements in health care delivery to low-income populations approaching those achieved through government intervention.

All these federal initiatives are based on the premise that equal opportunity can exist only when basic nutritional and health care needs are met in the formative years of development. If nutritional deficiencies or other health problems stunt intellectual and physical development in early childhood, compensatory programs are unlikely to erase the scars of initial deprivation. In this sense, the failure of free markets to guarantee equal opportunity for all members of American society is visible at the very beginning of the life cycle, imposing a cumulative burden on the least advantaged which often grows to insurmountable proportions.

Compensatory Education

By the time children enter kindergarten differences in family backgrounds have already been translated into a head start for some and a handicap for others. Repeated studies have found that children who come from low-income families or have parents with low levels of educational attainment are more likely to begin school with fewer cognitive skills than their more fortunate counterparts. Thus, the promotion of equal educational opportunity must reach down to preschool ages, lest those from the most adverse home environments fall hopelessly behind before the race for individual achievement formally begins.[6]

At the preschool level the primary federal program designed to remedy educational deficiencies associated with poverty has been Headstart. Providing a comprehensive set of educational, medical, and social services to poor preschool children and their families, local Headstart agencies seek to raise the basic cognitive skills of disadvantaged youngsters to the norms for their age. In most cases 80 percent of program costs are assumed by the federal government, funds being distributed to states according to an allotment formula based on prior expenditures, AFDC payments, and demographic data. As the largest public child care and development program, Headstart served nearly 400,000 children at a cost of $907 million in 1983, reaching roughly 20 percent of the four- and five-year-olds from low-income households who are eligible to participate in the program.

Since the creation of the Headstart program in 1965 a voluminous body of data and research has provided substantial evidence that Headstart positively influences nearly every aspect of early childhood development. Similar to federal interventions in child nutrition and preventive health care, early remedial efforts have been shown to be cost effective because they inhibit the development of more serious educational and behavioral problems. Longitudinal studies of Headstart indicate that by reducing the likelihood of later handicaps and repeated grades the program actually leads to a net reduction of public expenditures. The Children's Defense Fund estimated that Headstart's benefits outweigh its costs by reducing costs of special education services often associated with disadvantaged children who have not participated in Headstart.

Tangible results stemming from Headstart are as diverse as the multiple objectives of the program. Longitudinal surveys have found that Headstart children are less likely to enter special education classes and more likely to be in the correct grade for their age than those in control groups.[7] The U.S. Health and Human Services Department agency for children, youth, and families similarly concluded that cumulative improvements in cognitive skills are linked to Headstart participation, the most disadvantaged children enjoying the most positive effect.[8] In perhaps the most thorough analysis of early childhood programs researchers found that Headstart children were more likely than controls to graduate from high school, enroll in college, and obtain a self-supporting job; they were also less apt to be arrested or to register for welfare benefits. Based on these findings, the investigators estimated that taxpayers save nearly $5 in reduced crime, welfare, public education costs, and increased tax revenues for every $1 invested in preschool compensatory education programs.[9] The effectiveness of the Headstart approach has been partly responsible for the stability in its funding in a period of sweeping budget cuts.

For children already in school the most significant federal support for compensatory education is provided to local school districts under Chapter I (formerly Title I) of the Elementary and Secondary Education Act. Federal funds for Chapter I programs are distributed to local educational agencies according to a formula based on the number of children from low-income families residing in each school district. Limited federal aid is also provided to states for programs serving handicapped, migrant, neglected, and delinquent children. Congressional fiscal 1984 appropriations for Chapter I provided $3.5 billion for remedial instruction and related services at the primary level to school districts enrolling large numbers of poor children.

The magnitude of federal expenditures for educational aid provided under Title I prior to its revision in 1981 ensured that the program was among the most scrutinized and carefully evaluated social welfare initiatives. Because local administrators had considerable discretion in the use of Title I funds, effective monitoring of expenditures proved difficult, and the extent to which aid was targeted to low-income children was frequently challenged, especially in the early years of the program. Tension between the goals of targeted assistance and broad provision of service has been heightened in the new Chapter I statute, which allows states greater flexibility in the use of federal funds. While it is important to prevent counterproductive class segregation in local educational programs, the increasing possibility that many children benefiting from Chapter I expenditures will not be from poor households must be viewed with concern.

With safeguards to ensure appropriate use of federal funds for compensatory education, the original Title I program did narrow disparities in achievement between poor and nonpoor children. Evaluations of Title I conducted for the U.S. Department of Education found significant gains in achievement and educational attainment among low-income children over time.[10] The Title I program has been credited with eliminating over 40 percent of the difference in reading achievement between nine-year-old black and white children since its inception in 1965.[11] While Title I expenditures may have been too diluted in early years to produce measurable gains, this federal aid appears to have had a cumulative effect on the cognitive development and educational advancement of children from low-income households.

The rationale for federal aid to Indian education is similarly based on the serious deprivation suffered by native Americans living on federal reservations and other trust lands, including some of the nation's highest levels of poverty, unemployment, and substandard housing. In recognition of the federal government's culpability for the adverse conditions under which Indians live, as well as the importance of education in overcoming their historical disadvantages, federal funds have been allocated to Indian reservations, other local agencies educating Indians, and special programs for Indians in public schools. Fiscal year 1984 appropriations included $254 million to the Bureau of Indian Affairs for the operation of Indian-controlled boarding and day schools. An additional $69 million went to the Department of Education to support the education of Indian children in public schools. As a result of such efforts, gradual gains have been made in overcoming educational deficiencies, low enrollment, and poor performance. However, much work remains to be done to put Indian children on an equal footing with their peers.[12]

School Retention and Youth Employment

A few years later in the life cycle, those who enter their teens with cognitive skills and educational attainments lagging well behind their peers face a compounded set of problems. Compensatory education at an early age can rarely eliminate disparities in achievement between children from affluent and disadvantaged homes. By the time students reach junior high school the opportunity to lift the performance of the least successful to the norms of their age group has been all but lost, the underachievers having been identifed by educators as "slow" or unmotivated and finding little positive reinforcement in academic settings. The major challenge in promoting opportunity for disadvantaged youth becomes their retention in school for a period sufficient to establish their basic competency in the world of work.

The importance of educational attainment, and more specifically of a high school diploma or equivalency certificate, to occupational advancement and economic self-sufficiency has been clearly established. Years of schooling correlate positively with wages, earnings, income, employment rates, and occupational status. Students who have fallen far behind their peers in secondary schools have little chance of obtaining a postsecondary education and frequently enter the labor market without a high school diploma. Employers use educational attainment as a basis for screening job applicants, even in cases where skill requirements are not directly related to completion of a high school education. For these reasons government interventions designed to promote equal opportunity among youth have sought to keep the disadvantaged in school and to bolster the development of their basic skills.

The youth entitlement demonstration programs launched by the Carter administration provided a carefully structured experimental setting in which to examine the impact of subsidized employment on school attendance and test the feasibility of a job guarantee for disadvantaged youth. Implemented in seventeen cities between 1978 and 1980, the entitlement projects guaranteed part-time employment to some 76,000 low-income youths 16 to 19 years old living in designated poverty tracts on the condition that they remain in or return to school for a diploma or equivalency certificate. Although administered by local agencies, the pilot projects were supported totally with federal funds, and wage subsidies up to the full cost of wages and fringe benefits were authorized to encourage the participation of private employers in the program. The intent of the demonstration was twofold: first, to provide work experience and income to youth from impoverished households, and second, to use a guaranteed job as incentive for completion of a high school education.

The youth entitlement program refuted the oft-repeated assertion that it is not possible to fulfill an employment guarantee. Of the private businesses involved in the projects, 80 percent found the youth's work habits, attitudes, and willingness to work to be average or better. Furthermore, 75 percent of all private employers cited improved performance over time. Substantial support from the public and non-profit sectors insured the creation of a sufficient supply of jobs within relatively short amounts of time, thereby preserving the entitlement concept.[13] Considering the difficulties in altering behavior the results from the youth entitlement demonstrations were encouraging.[14]

In an immediate context the youth entitlement projects could provide the basis for a strong and sorely needed response to critical rates of minority youth unemployment. The Manpower Development Research Corporation, which evaluated the demonstration program, has estimated that a youth entitlement for eligible youth in the nation's designated poverty areas would cost about $700 million annually, and a universal program serving all low-income youth could be implemented for an estimated $1.7 billion. Expenditures of this magnitude, although sizable, fall well within the range of appropriations sustained for this purpose during the late 1970s. Given the severity of the youth unemployment problem and the potential of the entitlement concept for improving school attendance as well as employment rates among low-income teenagers, it is discouraging that this approach has yet to be incorporated in a permanent youth employment program.

The record of the youth entitlement demonstration projects also holds important lessons for long-term policies to expand the opportunities of disadvantaged youth. By linking job opportunities with education programs it is possible to both motivate low-income teenagers to continue their schooling and certify their competency for future employers. However, the key to success in this approach is reliance on an individualized course of instruction which avoids the frustrations encountered by underachieving youth in traditional classroom settings while permitting clear measures of student progress. When remedial programs are carefully structured around competency-based educational curricula, the available evidence suggests that disadvantaged youth can make substantial gains over relatively short periods.

Skill Training and Work Experience

For disadvantaged youth with the poorest educational prospects, skill training and work experience emerge as the most promising strategies for boosting future earnings and self-sufficiency. The potential gains from such interventions are significant but far from overwhelming. Federal training and work experience initiatives for low-income teenagers can facilitate their entry into the labor market, enhance the likelihood of steady employment in subsequent years, and generate marginal increases in future earnings. Yet the conservative ideal of equal opportunity provided through free markets is irrelevant by the time most disadvantaged youth join the labor force as their chances for career development and advancement have already been smothered under the collective weight of prior deprivations. At best, federal employment and training programs will mean the difference between poverty and modest incomes, between dependency and a firm attachment to work.

As federal training programs and numerous local initiatives funded under the Comprehensive Employment and Training Act (CETA) have demonstrated, government intervention can boost the employability of disadvantaged youth if careful attention is paid to program management and implementation. Evaluations of the Job Corps, an intensive residential program of remedial education, training, and work experience operated directly by the federal government since 1964, suggest that even the most disadvantaged youth can be helped through comprehensive federal initiatives. Focusing primarily on school dropouts aged sixteen through twenty-one in poor households, Job Corps is designed to remove youth from disruptive environments by placing them in residential centers with highly structured remedial programs.[15] The combination of basic education, occupational training, and an emphasis on more general living skills necessitates a substantial commitment of federal resources: in 1983 annual costs per slot averaged $15,000.

Because Job Corps serves the most disadvantaged of low-income youth rather than selecting the most employable among eligible youth at the outset, the rate of attrition in the program is high. A 1977 profile of Job Corps participants conveys the magnitude of the challenge: five of six were school dropouts averaging below sixth grade reading and math levels; only one-half came from two-parent families; the typical family size of enrollees was nearly twice the national average; and the per capita family income of corpsmembers was less than one-third that of the mean for the total population. Four of ten participants had previous arrests (of those, three-fourths had prior convictions), and more than one-third of all 1977 participants had never held a job with at least twenty hours per week for longer than a month. Not surprisingly, only a portion of this trouble-plagued client population is willing and able to complete the Job Corps program: for every ten entrants only three have managed to complete vocational training.

Corpsmembers who complete training enjoy consider-able gains in postprogram employment. Males who finished the vocational program in 1977 earned $1,250 more annually than experimental controls twelve to eighteen months after termination; the annual increase in earnings for females averaged $1,500.[16] These gains resulted almost exclusively from higher postprogram employment rates rather than higher wage rates, and overall earnings for completers were enhanced by substantial increases in military enlistment among participants as compared to control groups. The Job Corps program generally heightened the attachment of disadvantaged youth to the labor force while also raising their ability to meet entry requirements of private employers and the armed services.

Unlike many nonresidential supported work programs, Job Corps also has produced distinct behavioral shifts among participants. Self-esteem increased and family relations im-proved for those who remained in the program for at least ninety days. Reduced child bearing and out-of-wedlock births, increased mobility, and more frequent matriculation in college and postsecondary education have similarly been linked to Job Corps participation. Most importantly for taxpayers supporting the program, corpsmembers have proved far less likely to engage in criminal activities than their nonparticipating counterparts. In the first year following completion of the program the arrest rate for 1,977 participants was 35 percent lower than that of control groups. These salutary effects of enrollment in Job Corps contributed to societal benefits at least equal to the value of earnings gains derived from classroom training.[17]

The remedial instruction that is an integral component of the comprehensive Job Corps approach provides further testament to the importance of self-paced educational programs for disadvantaged youth discussed previously. Notwithstanding their demonstrated difficulty in traditional classroom settings, corpsmembers respond more positively to individualized instruction with standardized competency-based testing. Entering with less than a sixth-grade average reading level, participants gain an average 1.5 years of competency in 90 hours of instruction and 2.2 years in 150 hours.[18] This success in strengthening the basic educational abilities of poor school dropouts offers encouraging evidence that self-paced programs with clearly measured standards of progress can motivate the most disadvantaged students and facilitate their educational achievement.

The provision of supervised work experience is of greatest assistance to youth struggling to enter the labor market, but it can also aid low-income adults for whom lack of a prior work record poses a major obstacle to employment. In the national supported work demonstration project conducted between 1974 and 1979, individuals with poor employment prospects were placed for twelve to eighteen months in jobs in which their performance was closely supervised, work standards were gradually increased over time, and peer group support was emphasized. The demonstration focused on four target groups: women with a history of welfare dependency, ex-addicts, ex-offenders, and young school dropouts. Supported work offered no training to participants and limited the duration of subsidized employment regardless of whether individuals had been placed in other jobs. With an elaborate experimental design, the program was structured explicitly to test the impact of a supportive work experience on future employability.

For those with limited work experience who lack the discipline, work habits, or record of employment necessary to compete in the labor market, supported work demonstrated that provision of a supervised job itself can reduce barriers to employment among some disadvantaged groups. The clearest successes were achieved in projects serving women with dependent children who had long records of welfare dependency. After an average stay in supported work of nine months, welfare mothers worked more and earned higher wage rates than controls who had not participated in the program. The long-term social benefits of increased employment and reduced dependency outweighed the costs of this government intervention, including day care services, supervision, and peer counseling, by an estimated $8,000 per AFDC program participant (1976 dollars) over a twenty-seven-month period.[19]

Supervised work experience is by no means a panacea for the employment problems of the disadvantaged. Although relatively successful in facilitating the entry of welfare mothers into the labor market, supported work had little effect on the employment and earnings of ex-addicts, ex-offenders, or school dropouts. The program did lead to reductions in the criminal activity of ex-addicts, but similar shifts were not identified among other target groups. The supported work approach appears most promising for low-income persons with the least amount of prior work experience and the fewest complicating behavioral problems.

Equal Access and Advancement

Not all low-income teenagers are candidates for remedial education and occupational training. Quite the opposite is true. Despite their relative deprivation many poor youth find the support, guidance, and motivation necessary to succeed in school and compete effectively with their more affluent peers. Others have the potential for sustained academic achievement, but need modest encouragement and support in order to develop their innate abilities. For these low-income youth equal opportunity for advancement is promoted by ensuring that they have appropriate models for academic achievement and the financial resources to further their education.

Higher education has been perceived by low-income Americans as an important means of upward social mobility, a belief sustained by the higher incomes and steadier employment enjoyed by college graduates. During the 1960s the civil rights movement similarly raised the aspirations of many blacks and other minorities who sought to escape poverty with a college degree. The TRIO programs—including Upward Bound, Talent Search, and other special services for disadvantaged students—have served potential college students from poor households since 1965, offering remedial instruction and tutoring, personal counseling, and career development services to promising youth in need of such assistance. To be eligible for TRIO services participants must be from families with incomes not exceeding 150 percent of the federal poverty threshold ($10,200 for a family of four in 1983), and neither parent may be a college graduate. Over 500,000 students were enrolled in these federal programs in fiscal 1983, with expenditures totaling $155 million.

Hampered by budget restrictions that enable them to serve only a small fraction of the eligible population, TRIO programs have nonetheless produced some encouraging results. Nearly six of every ten Upward Bound high school graduates have entered college. More importantly, at least 60 percent of those who enrolled in college in 1976 were still in attendance two years later, indicating that Upward Bound students are as likely to remain in college as are students from more affluent backgrounds. Talent Search and related projects have been similarly successful, often placing between 75 and 90 percent of their students in postsecondary institutions.[20] The House Committee on Education and Labor estimated that

20 percent of all college minority freshmen in 1982 were placed by federally supported projects.[21] Despite the inability of these programs to overcome large educational deficiencies from earlier years, they are effective mechanisms for bolstering student motivation and providing the extra support necessary to guide poor youth into postsecondary education.

The success of the TRIO programs must be shared with federal student assistance programs, which have been expanded steadily since the late 1960s. Federal grant, loan, and work-study programs for low- and middle-income students have dramatically reduced financial barriers to a college education, reaching over 9 million students in 1983. Although the Reagan administration opposed increases in federal student aid expenditures, its assault on social spending has not led to sizable reductions in this politically popular area due to strong congressional support. The $4 billion devoted to needbased financial aid for students in fiscal year 1984 is essential for college attendance among low-income youth.

The cornerstone of federal support for low-income students in postsecondary education is the Pell grant (formerly the basic educational opportunity grant) program. Enacted in 1972, outlays from this program increased rapidly through the late 1970s, reaching $2.8 billion in 1983. Of the nearly 3 million college students from low-income families receiving awards up to $1,800 in 1983, 70 percent were from families with annual incomes below $12,000, and 57 percent were minority students. Federal student aid played a key role in boosting college attendance by low-income youth from 3 to 5 percent of total college enrollment between 1974 and 1981, even though an increasing portion of aid flowed to middle- and upper-income students during this period.[22]

Equality under the Law

Job discrimination has long been one of the major causes of poverty and most obvious barriers to advancement in the labor market. Black and other minority workers suffer higher unemployment rates and have lower labor force participation rates than whites. When out of work they face dispropor- tionately longer periods of unemployment; when employed they are concentrated in low-wage occupations. Beginning with adoption of Title VII of the Civil Rights Act of 1964 and the creation of the Equal Employment Opportunity Com- mission to enforce its provisions, the federal government has played an important role in bolstering the economic prospects of minorities and prompted slow progress toward a society in which opportunities for employment and advancement can- not be denied on the basis of sex, race, color, or national origin. Although individual prejudice may persist, govern- ment intervention can alter the institutional biases that render discrimination so pervasive, including unequal access to education and training, occupational segregation, and barriers to advancement beyond entry-level positions.

The federal drive for equal opportunity spawned by the civil rights movement of the 1950s and 1960s has brought significant progress in ameliorating wage and employment discrimination. Between 1968 and 1982 the average income of two-earner black families rose from 73.2 percent to 84.8 percent of that for comparable white households.[23] Similarly, the gap between the median weekly earnings of black full- time wage and salary workers and white ones narrowed from 74 percent in 1970 to 80 percent in 1981.[24] However, these gains have not reduced income disparities between all black and white families due to a disproportionate increase in the number of female-headed black households in recent years. Adjusted 1980 data that control for changes in family composition during the 1970s reveal that, in the absence of such changes, the ratio of black to white median family income would have risen from 61 percent in 1970 to 66 percent in 1980, rather than falling to 55 percent as it actually had by 1982.[25] This evidence suggests that federal antidis- crimination efforts, along with investments in education and other social programs, have contributed to a slow rise in the earnings of black workers relative to their white counterparts.

Federal equal employment initiatives are also in part responsible for the gradually expanding access of black workers to better-paying occupations with possibilities for career advancement. Between 1972 and 1981 the proportion of employed minority professionals rose from 7.2 to 9.9 percent. Among managers and administrators this ratio climbed from 4 to 5.8 percent, and among skilled craft workers it rose from 6.9 to 8.5 percent.[26] Minorities continue to be underrepresented in these favored occupations, constituting 11.6 percent of the total workforce in 1981, and they remain disproportionately concentrated in low-skilled clerical, service, and blue-collar occupations. Yet these modest improvements in occupational distribution for blacks, representing increases in their share of employment in professional and skilled occupations ranging from 23 to 50 percent in the course of a decade, demonstrate the impact of equal employment and affirmative action programs championed at the federal level.

The gains of the civil rights movement have been most visible in advancing political participation among blacks. As a result of the Voting Rights Act of 1965, millions of black citizens have registered to vote, rendering them a powerful political force in many parts of the country. The number of black elected officials at all levels of government has risen from 1,472 in 1970 to 5,606 in 1983, including 248 black mayors representing over 20 million Americans suggesting the growing political clout of blacks. Another forty-seven U.S. cities, including San Antonio, Denver, Miami, and Tampa, now have Hispanic mayors. Although systemic efforts to deny minorities access to the polls persist in some areas, the outrage provoked by discrimination against black voters itself reveals the progress of the past two decades. Federal intervention has been instrumental in opening the doors to more equal political participation regardless of race or national origin.

The advances brought by federal action have materialized slowly, and significant portions of minority populations are still excluded from mainstream America. An economic portrait of black America conveys the urgency of a renewed commitment to equal economic opportunity. In 1982 the median income of black families was 55.3 percent of that for white families, virtually the same disparity which existed in 1960. The poverty rate for black families stood at 33 percent in 1982, compared to 9.6 percent for white families. Differences in educational attainment, although contributing to the income gap between blacks and whites, do not fully account for it. A recent analysis of the economic status of black Americans found that family incomes for households headed by black college graduates parallels the income distribution for white families whose heads have completed only a high school education.[27] Clearly, this discouraging evidence indicates that until more vigorous and sustained legal assaults on discrimination are undertaken, the promise of equal opportunity will remain unfulfilled. The persistence of deprivation and disadvantage in the black community also suggests that equal opportunity statutes are necessary but not sufficient ingredients of a comprehensive strategy for bolstering the economic prospects of the least fortunate.[28]

Relief for the Unemployed

Beyond its antidiscrimination efforts the federal government pursues few avenues to expanded opportunity for citizens in the middle stages of life. Its primary assistance to disadvantaged adults focuses on meeting basic needs through income transfers and the provision of food, shelter, energy, and health care. This income support, by far the most expensive component of the modern welfare system, is an essential response to the hardships confronting those who are forced into idleness. It allows the unemployed to keep body and soul together but does little to promote equal opportunity. The fulfillment of basic needs represents a last resort for adults who have failed to discover a path to self-sufficiency, an acknowledgment that for some the cumulative burden of a lifetime of deprivation is too great to reverse through federal interventions.

For qualified workers, a loss of income resulting from involuntary unemployment is partially offset by programs providing temporary wage replacement. The state-administered programs normally pay benefits for a maximum of 26 weeks, with weekly benefits averaging $121 in 1983. Although 97 percent of all wage and salary workers are covered by the system, less than half of the unemployed qualify for benefits while temporarily out of work. Reasons for disqualification include lack of sufficient prior employment or earnings, voluntary quit, dismissal for just cause, and refusal to accept suitable work. In addition to the regular 26 weeks of benefits, the system has provided extended income support during recessions. In fiscal 1983 the state-administered program plus the federally-mandated added benefits amounted to $30 billion.

Marginal improvements in employment and earnings for unemployed adults are generally sought through federal employment and training initiatives. In providing work experience or compensating for job shortages, public employment programs offer an alternative form of income maintenance, meeting basic needs but contributing little to the skills and future employability of participants. Federal training efforts, on the other hand, have proved successful in raising employability and increasing the access of low-income adults to occupations that would otherwise be closed to them. For most adults with limited skills and deficient education, federal intervention can modestly enhance prospects for employment at a decent wage.

Though limited the effectiveness of federal training programs has been well documented. Exhaustive longitudinal surveys of participants in federally supported training programs have found that on-the-job training raised postprogram earnings by 18 percent over those of comparison groups, classroom training resulted in a 10 percent increase in the first year following participation, and participants in public service employment experienced a 7 percent increase in their post-enrollment earnings compared to a control group. Every dollar invested in on-the-job training returned an estimated $2.55 in social benefits, and a similar investment in classroom training returned $1.38 to society.[29] Because federal taxpayers bear the cost of training and earnings gains accrue directly to participants, the benefit-cost ratio for training from a narrow taxpayer's perspective is considerably lower, accounting in part for the tenuous political support lent to these activities. Still, when measured against realistic objectives and expectations, the evidence suggests that federally-sponsored training expands employment opportunities for individuals and provides positive returns on investment for society.

Participants in employment and training programs benefit from services that cannot be separated out when their post-training income is measured. Particularly encouraging is the record achieved in providing basic education. Typically, ninety hours of adult instruction results in a 1.5 year achievement gain in reading ability and 1 year in math. Computer assisted instruction, pioneered by Job Corps centers, doubled those gain rates. The English as a second language (ESL) program has had especially high payoffs. People with substantial skills which they are unable to apply because of language deficiencies are freed from that bondage in a short low-cost ESL program.

As concern mounts over declines in manufacturing employment, training programs increasingly may play a role in facilitating adjustment to economic change as well as broadening opportunities for individual advancement. Although the pace and scope of economic transitions fueled by international competition and technological advance remain unclear, the problems facing affected workers are and will continue to be substantial. Workers in traditional manufacturing industries tend to have limited education and narrow skills, leaving them with little flexibility, few transferable skills or job-search experience to pursue new occupations or careers when layoffs lead to permanent displacement. For workers unlikely to be recalled to their former jobs, federal adjustment and retraining programs may be the only alternative to prolonged periods of unemployment and financial hardship.

Despite the lack of a comprehensive federal policy addressing the needs of displaced workers, evidence from programs in other industrial nations suggests that government-sponsored retraining and adjustment efforts can boost reemployment rates among affected workers and thereby help defuse public resistance to economic change. Similar initiatives in this country have received limited funding, but early evaluations of projects funded by the federally funded displaced workers program indicate the potential benefits of such efforts.[30] Given the seriously depressed condition of many communities battered by plant closings and layoffs, these preliminary findings offer encouragement for a more thorough, national response to the problems of displaced workers.[31]

Dignity in Retirement

At the end of the life cycle federal policy has long been directed toward the provision of income security in retirement. With the expectation to work largely lifted from individuals after age sixty-five, the federal focus on opportunity shifts from employment and occupational advancement to providing basic income for the "golden years." Through development of the social security and public and private pension systems, government interventions have been highly successful in breaking the link between old age and poverty during the postwar era. By 1982 older Americans were less likely to live in poverty (14.6 percent) than were their younger counterparts—a sharp contrast to the situation a generation ago, when the national poverty rate stood at 22 percent, but 35 percent of those over sixty-five resided in households with incomes below the poverty line.

The effectiveness of federal aid to older Americans can be traced to the combination of income transfers and in-kind assistance to meet basic needs. Payments under social security have grown rapidly, and a steadily rising proportion of the aged population (94 percent in 1980) receives retirement benefits. Pension benefits for indigent veterans provide additional income security in old age. Nonetheless, the dramatic advances toward fulfilling basic needs in retirement would not have been possible without health insurance coverage for the elderly through Medicare. Entitlements and supportive services have responded directly to the threats of infirmity and dependency which accompany old age, thereby heightening opportunities for dignity and self-sufficiency in the final years of life.

The broad political consensus in support of aid to the elderly which has fueled past gains may never be achieved in other federal efforts to eradicate poverty. Posing none of the conflicts with work that plague direct assistance to younger segments of the population, old-age benefits are generally perceived as earned and well deserved. The fact that we all strive to achieve old age also contributes to the popularity of federal programs that promote a decent income in retirement. Other groups especially vulnerable to deprivation enjoy neither the aura of deservedness nor the roots of shared experience which generate broad political support for aid to the elderly from all social classes. In this sense the substantial improvement of economic well-being after age sixty-five demonstrates both the efficacy of federal intervention and the potential for substantial progress against poverty at all ages if a more compassionate understanding of its nature and causes develops in American society.

PRAGMATIC CHOICES AND POLITICAL REALITIES

This comprehensive, although not universal, network of federal social programs has made great progress over the past fifty years in alleviating deprivation in the United States. The documented successes of federal intervention demonstrate that age-old social and economic pathologies can indeed be altered to pave the way to greater self-sufficiency for those formerly excluded from a productive and rewarding life and to provide expanded opportunities for others. However, many social problems have proved more pervasive and persistent than was originally thought, requiring more varied strategies for their amelioration and more realistic criteria by which to gauge success or failure. In addition, the process of change has sometimes generated unwanted side effects, posing new problems for policymakers. Fundamentally, these problems are the natural by-products of any attempts to implement new processes and construct new institutions. They should not be allowed to obscure past gains, and they should not be used as an excuse to abandon the struggle for social progress.[32]

Nonetheless, in a political context the realization that there are no easy answers or quick one-shot solutions to problems of poverty and long-term dependency has created profound problems for the welfare system. Repeatedly, from the New Deal through the Great Society, policymakers have clung to the hope that the need for government aid to the poor would dissipate, if not within a few years then over the course of a generation or two. The authors of the original Social Security Act in 1935 presumed that the need for public assistance would wither away as younger workers became fully covered by social insurance—an expectation that was shattered by steadily expanding welfare rolls since World War II. Similarly, a central premise of the war on poverty was that investments in education and training, civil rights protections, and community organization could dramatically lift this generation's poor out of deprivation and ensure their children a decent life. Cycles of poverty and dependency have proved considerably more intractable than Lyndon Johnson anticipated when he proclaimed that, "for the first time in world history, we have the abundance and the ability to free every man from hopeless want, and to free every person to find fulfillment in the works of his mind or the labor of his hands."[33]

When government interventions are successful, their beneficial effects tend to be cumulative and long term. The political implications of this lesson are troublesome, but they cannot be avoided in the development of the modern welfare system. Because effective aid to the poor requires a combination of targeted assistance to individuals, institutional change, economic development, and appropriate macroeconomic policies, public investments must be maintained over prolonged periods in order to improve prospects for self-sufficiency appreciably and permanently. The anticipation of visible instant success is strong among elected officials as well as taxpayers. Comprehensive, long-term approaches to welfare efforts have therefore been extremely difficult to sustain or defend from political challenge. The legacy of the Great Society vividly illustrates the dilemma: federal initiatives in some cases produced little positive result due to an insufficient commitment of funds over too brief a period of time; in other cases promising strategies were misjudged as failures because they were slow in generating visible, short-term gains.

The political urge to equate high program costs with waste and inefficiency has also hampered the implementation and expansion of federal programs that carry a steep price tag even if their effectiveness and social benefits have been demonstrated. While outreach costs and the difficulties in motivating targeted groups obviously must be taken into account, the lack of sufficient funding has played a key role in the limited success of federal interventions. Programs with high initial start-up costs, long-term or comprehensive approaches, and delayed benefits have proved most vulnerable to the budget ax, despite proven success or strong expectations of significant net benefits. A shortage of funds and political patience has done the injustice of too often branding otherwise successful ventures as failures.

Conflicts between long-term investments in social welfare and short-term political pressures are heightened by the complexity of barriers to economic opportunity and the difficulty of constructing effective approaches to social problems. The experience during recent decades suggests that the federal government must proceed on several fronts simultaneously if it is to be successful in alleviating poverty or reducing dependency. For example, training of low-income workers is not likely to have a significant impact on overall poverty levels or welfare caseloads if provided amid high unemployment or in declining geographical areas unless suitable employment and economic development programs are also initiated and the segmentation of labor markets overcome. Although income transfers address the immediate needs of the poor, they do not result in lasting improvements in the earnings capacity and self-sufficiency of beneficiaries unless they are complemented by public efforts designed to enhance the skills of the recipients and the institutions that trap them in poverty. As a result of the interdependence of federal strategies, individual initiatives viewed in isolation can appear to have failed because concomitant interventions necessary for their success were not undertaken. At the same time, the interaction of these seemingly disparate programs can yield results far in excess of the potential of isolated efforts.

One of the clearest lessons of federal social welfare experience is that poverty cannot be eliminated solely through a reliance on income transfers. Income maintenance certainly must be a central component of any approach in aid of the poor, but a strategy relying on transfers alone cannot enhance self-sufficiency and irreconcilably conflicts with the functioning of the labor market. In a society in which wages for millions of workers are too low to lift them out of poverty, the provision of adequate cash assistance to the nonworking poor, if unaccompanied by incentives to supplement assistance with earnings, inevitably raises serious questions of equity and generates strong political opposition among taxpayers. In addition, income transfers large enough to lift low-income households above the poverty threshold, if not tied to work effort, would trigger large drops in labor force participation or force massive public expenditures to the nonpoor in order to preserve acceptable work incentives. These political and economic realities have led to the demise of successive guaranteed income schemes during the past two decades and demonstrate the need for federal strategies that link work and welfare so as to assist both the working and dependent poor.

In the 1960s and 1970s federal policymakers, regardless of party affiliation, partially avoided the conflicts of income maintenance by extending in-kind assistance to the working poor. Food stamps, school nutrition programs, subsidized housing, and, in some states, health care coverage were made available to low-wage earners as well as welfare recipients, thereby raising the living standards of all poor Americans. The desire to target benefits to the most needy and to limit program costs has presented low-wage workers with high marginal tax rates and some of the corresponding work disincentives found in income maintenance programs. However, in-kind aid does not provide the disposable income that most directly undermines work motivation and has offered a politically acceptable means of supplementing the incomes of the working poor as well as the dependent poor.

In-kind assistance is an essential part of any comprehensive response to the needs of the poor. This fulfillment of basic needs not only arouses less public animosity than cash assistance but also responds to social problems arising out of specific market inadequacies. Cash assistance in amounts equal to federal expenditures on in-kind aid often could not ensure the availability of supply or appropriate distribution of essential goods and services. When free markets would otherwise provide an inadequate supply of goods or services, public provision through the use of subsidies or direct intervention is clearly necessary. Marginal cash assistance distributed to the poor for housing, for example, is more likely to raise rents than increase the supply of shelter. Similarly, in the case of health care, where individual needs vary widely among those with identical incomes, in-kind assistance secures the necessities of life for all regardless of differing personal circumstances.

Success in reconciling conflicts between income maintenance and the functioning of the labor market will require greater ease of movement between work and welfare and new mechanisms for combining these sources of support. In the past, refusal to acknowledge that the meager returns of unskilled labor lie at the heart of the poverty problem has precluded adoption of policies that would reflect the need to combine work with welfare. Popular wisdom has preserved the traditional belief that work provides an escape from dependency and a path to self-sufficiency, despite conclusive evidence that work effort brings no such guarantee, particularly for large families. Hence, the federal role in social welfare repeatedly has been based on sharp distinctions between the employable and the dependent poor that mask the reality of millions who can work—full time, part time, or intermittently—but cannot earn enough to escape from poverty. As already noted, half of the adult poor are in the labor force.

Future approaches that seek to integrate work and welfare will require a reexamination of society's definition of the deserving poor and of appropriate federal roles in social welfare. Sound approaches for combining work and welfare already can be found in rudimentary form in the federal earned income tax credit, supported work and other wage subsidy experiments, health care coverage for the medically needy, and AFDC benefits for households with unemployed fathers. However, opposition to the expansion of wage subsidies and in-kind assistance to the working poor is likely to be strong—a reflection of the belief that earnings are and should be based on an individual's market worth.

Federal social welfare initiatives operate within broad political and economic constraints. The experience since the 1930s clearly indicates the inherent tensions between targeting of benefits and the political acceptability of government programs. Without question, universal provision of basic services engenders broad public acceptance and a strong base of political support, as illustrated by the evolution of social security, Medicare, and college loan programs. Yet the extension of aid regardless of income necessarily increases the cost of government interventions, diluting their impact on the most needy and subjecting federal roles to challenge as inappropriate or extravagant. On the other hand, as a major architect of social legislation, Wilbur Cohen, has observed, efforts for poor people inevitably become poor programs. The conflict between targeting and universality can never be fully resolved; the challenge in the development of federal social programs is to strike a balance that gives every American a stake in the modern welfare system while focusing the necessary resources on those who need them most with due regard to the dignity of recipients.

In theory, the Reagan administration's attempt to focus federal aid on those with greatest need has some legitimacy. Although judgments regarding the appropriate degree of targeting are always difficult, a strong case could be made by 1980 that too large a share of scarce federal resources were being diverted into benefits for the non-needy. The tragedy of the Reagan program is that the criteria of more narrowly focused aid has been applied in a highly selective, rather than a comprehensive and equitable, fashion. To be sure, eligibility in means-tested programs has been restricted, targeting aid to the poorest of low-income households. Yet in a broader context, the Reagan administration has not made a serious effort to curtail federal aid to the non-needy through a host of special-interest subsidies and universal entitlements, and its spending reductions have fallen most heavily on exactly those programs designed to serve the truly needy.

Social programs that provide targeted assistance to low-income persons generally carry the stigma of welfare and rest on a fragile base of political support. They have a narrow constituency with little political clout to preserve their funding during periods of austerity, resentment, or retrenchment. The experience of recent decades has demonstrated the need for efforts to organize disadvantaged groups, both as a counter-vailing force against beneficiaries of the status quo and as the institutional foundation for enhanced self-sufficiency. In the absence of community-based organizations and decisionmaking processes which provide a voice for the poor, recipients of targeted federal assistance are neither assured the political representation to protect their interests nor given the opportunity to marshall local resources for their own benefit.

Effective community organization can heighten the impact of individualized assistance by altering the underlying institutional barriers which limit prospects for advancement among the poor. The community action agencies authorized by the Economic Opportunity Act of 1964, while controversial, illustrated the importance of local organizations that represent the poor. These public and private agencies clearly have influenced the allocation of government resources to social programs, rendering them more responsive to those they serve. By involving poor recipients in the planning and operation of such programs, community action agencies have often provoked the ire of local officials with challenges to established patterns of decisionmaking and social service delivery. Nonetheless, they have been instrumental in developing and coordinating social programs in low-income areas and acting as advocate agencies for the poor.

No federal social program can hope to survive and succeed without public support. Yet programs serving the poor face the greatest perils. If structured to make lasting changes in poor communities and the institutions which serve them, federal initiatives threaten established interests and quickly generate their own opposition. If unaccompanied by fundamental institutional changes which guarantee sustained support, government interventions are vulnerable to the charge that they offer only temporary relief without long term or permanent gains.

Political leaders can play a crucial role in either promoting or undermining the needed consensus for continued social progress. Given the inevitability of pragmatic choices and political compromises in the development of new social welfare policies, the test of leadership lies in the ability to preserve a vision of the common good and to inspire public commitment to societal goals. Regrettably, failed leadership has used the nation's poor economic performance during the past decade as an excuse for rejecting laudable Great Society goals. The ensuing retrenchment is a sobering reminder that the role we choose for government profoundly affects the opportunities of future generations and the social fabric of the nation.

NOTES

1. Lyndon B. Johnson, June 26, 1964.
2. Sar A. Levitan, *Programs in Aid of the Poor for the 1980s* (Baltimore, Md.: Johns Hopkins University Press, 1980).
3. Kristin A. Moore et al., *Teenage Motherhood: Social and Economic Consequences* (Washington, D.C.: The Urban Institute, 1979); Kristin A. Moore, Margaret Simms, and Charles Betsy, *Information Services and Aspirations: Race Differences in Adolescent Fertility* (Washington, D.C.: The Urban Institute, 1984).
4. Julius B. Richmond, testimony before the U.S. Congress, House Subcommittee on Elementary, Secondary, and Vocational Education, September 21, 1982.
5. Children's Defense Fund, "A Children's Defense Budget: An Analysis of the President's FY 1984 Budget and Children" (Washington, D.C.: Children's Defense Fund, February 1983), p. 39.
6. Sar A. Levitan, *The Great Society's Poor Law* (Baltimore, Md.: Johns Hopkins University Press, 1969), Chapter 4.
7. Irving Lazar and Richard Darlington, "Lasting Effects of Early Education: A Report from the Consortium for Longitudinal Studies,"

Monographs of the Society for Research in Child Development (Ithaca, N.Y.: Cornell University, 1982).

8. Raymond Collins, "Headstart: Foundation for Excellence," The Administration for Children, Youth and Families (U.S. Department of Health and Human Services, 1983), pp. 11–13.

9. David P. Weikart, "The Cost Effectiveness of High Quality Early Childhood Programs" (Testimony before the U.S. Congress, House Select Committee on Children, Youth and Families, June 30, 1983).

10. Henry Zagorski et al., "Overview of Report 12: Does Compensatory Education Narrow the Achievement Gap?" *Study of the Sustaining Effects of Compensatory Education on Basic Skills* (Santa Monica, Ca.: System Development Corporation, December 1981); Judith Anderson and Robert Stonehill, *A Report to Congress: An Evaluation of the Elementary and Secondary Education Act Title I Program Operations and Educational Effects*, Office of Planning, Budget and Education, U.S. Department of Education (Washington, D.C.: U.S. Department of Education, March 1982).

11. Children's Defense Fund, "A Children's Defense Budget," p. 39.

12. Sar A. Levitan and William B. Johnston, *Indian Giving: Federal Programs for Native Americans* (Baltimore, Md.: Johns Hopkins University Press, 1975), pp. 34–48.

13. William Diaz et al., *Linking School and Work for Disadvantaged Youths: The YIEPP Demonstration: Final Implementation Report* (New York: Manpower Demonstration Research Corporation, 1982).

14. George Farkas et al., *Impacts from the Youth Incentive Entitlement Pilot Projects: Participation, Work and Schooling Over the Full Program Period* (New York: Manpower Demonstration Research Corporation, December 1982).

15. Sar A. Levitan and Benjamin H. Johnston, *The Job Corps: A Social Experiment That Works* (Baltimore, Md.: Johns Hopkins University Press, 1975); Job Corps in Brief, Fiscal 1980 (Washington, D.C.: U.S. Employment and Training Administration, 1981); Charles Mallar et al., *The Lasting Impacts of Job Corps Participation* (Washington, D.C.: U.S. Government Printing Office, 1980).

16. Robert Taggart, *A Fisherman's Guide: An Assessment of Training and Remediation Strategies* (Kalamazoo, Mich.: W.E. Upjohn Institute for Employment Research, 1981), pp. 282–86.

17. Mathematica, *Evaluation of the Economic Impact of the Job Corps Programs* (Princeton, N.J.: Mathematica, 1978).

18. Robert Taggart, *A Fisherman's Guide*, p. 287.

19. P. Kemper, D. Long, and C. Thornton, *The Supported Work Evaluation: Final Benefit-Cost Analysis* (New York: Manpower Development Research Corporation, 1980).

20. Paul L. Franklin, "A Study of Talent Search and Educational Opportunity Centers" (Washington, D.C.: The College Board, October 4, 1983).
21. W.A. Blakey et al, "Briefing For Members of U.S. Congress, House Committee on Education and Labor and New Members of Congress" (Washington, D.C.: U.S. Government Printing Office, January 1983).
22. National Commission on Student Financial Assistance, "Changes in College Participation Rates and Student Financial Assistance: 1969, 1974, 1981" (Washington, D.C.: Applied Systems Institute, Inc., January 28, 1983).
23. U.S. Department of Commerce, Bureau of the Census, *Money Income and Poverty Status of Families and Persons in the United States: 1982*, Series P60, No. 140, July 1983, p. 11; *Consumer Income*, No. 101, January 1976, p. 27.
24. U.S. Department of Commerce, Bureau of the Census, *Statistical Abstract of the United States: 1982–83*, p. 404.
25. U.S. Department of Commerce, Bureau of the Census, *Changing Family Composition and Income Differentials*, Special Demographic Analyses CDS-80-7, 1982, p. 12.
26. U.S. Department of Commerce, Bureau of the Census, *Statistical Abstract of the United States: 1982–83*, pp. 388–90.
27. "A Dream Deferred: The Economic Status of Black Americans" (Washington, D.C.: The Center for the Study of Social Policy, July 1983), p. 14.
28. Sar A. Levitan, William Johnston and Robert Taggart, *Still A Dream* (Cambridge, Mass.: Harvard University Press, 1975), pp. 13–43, 331–56.
29. Robert Taggart, *A Fisherman's Guide*, p. 283.
30. Abt Associates Inc., *The Downriver Community Conference Economic Readjustment Activity Program: Impact Findings from the First Phase of Operations*, (Boston: Abt Associates Inc., May 20, 1983), pp. 5–8.
31. National Council on Employment Policy, "The Displaced Worker in American Society: An Overdue Policy Issue" (Washington, D.C.: The Council, February 1983); U.S. Department of Labor, "Plant Closings: What Can Be Learned from Best Practice," (Washington, D.C.: U.S. Government Printing Office, 1982).
32. Sar A. Levitan and Robert Taggart, *The Promise of Greatness* (Cambridge, Mass.: Harvard University Press, 1976), pp. 3–30.
33. Lyndon B. Johnson, June 26, 1964, on signing the Economic Opportunity Act.

6

A Renewed Quest for Opportunity

I think we need a new dialogue in America.... It's time to bury the myth that bigger Government brings more opportunity and compassion.[1]

—Ronald Reagan

The test of our progress is not whether we add more to the abundance of those who have much; it is whether we provide enough for those who have too little.[2]

—Franklin D. Roosevelt

The lessons of more than four decades offer the basis for a constructive revision of the American welfare state in the 1980s. Regrettably, the political climate during the past several years has shifted gradually but steadily from refinement to retrenchment in federal social welfare policy. A number of the factors that contributed to this mood of retrenchment—particularly the sense of economic insecurity spawned by OPEC oil price hikes and the decline in productivity growth, resulting in stagnation of real wages—were beyond the control of policymakers. Yet the severity of the nation's retreat from federal responsibility has been dramatically compounded by President Reagan's readiness to offer government as a scapegoat for economic turmoil and by many liberals' capitulation in the face of this antigovernment ideology.

Although a careful examination of priorities is essential in a time of slow economic growth and the need to retrench on some efforts is necessary, the nation has gone beyond restraint and reassessment to embrace a debilitating cynicism regarding the appropriate roles and capacities of government. Rather than evaluating federal activities and responsibilities on their merits, politicians intimidated by highly publicized antigovernment sentiments, as reflected in presumed tax revolts, have found it tempting to "run against Washington" and to question federal roles in social welfare. Few have had the political courage to challenge the conservative thesis that federal intervention was the primary cause of the nation's apparent economic decline. Sharing the public's fears of a disintegrating economy, cowed Democrats have joined Republicans in halting and partially reversing the social progress engendered by the modern welfare system.

By acquiescing to the notion that America suffers from an excess of government intervention and regulation, liberals have allowed President Reagan to dominate the social welfare agenda and abdicate federal responsibilities for promoting opportunity and social justice. The damage wrought by the Reagan program is already evident. Poverty rates have risen sharply, the social welfare safety net has been unraveled, and the distribution of income has been skewed in favor of the most affluent. Notwithstanding President Reagan's rhetoric, the administration has offered nothing new. Although the supply-side theories of the Reagan administration were packaged in novel ways, they served, in the words of David Stockman, who masterminded the Reagan 1981 tax and budget cuts, merely as a "Trojan horse" for adoption of the "trickle-down" policies that have long been part of conservative ideology.[3]

The inequities and hardship imposed by Reagan's economic and social policies reflect the immediate costs of withdrawal and retrenchment. The more lasting legacy of his administration may lie in its persistent efforts to undermine public confidence in government. In some instances existing social welfare initiatives may be strengthened by limiting the scope of federal intervention and placing greater reliance upon market mechanisms. In most cases, however, an insistence upon less government deprives federal policymakers of the means by which to redress grievances and alter market deficiencies. If the American people accept Reagan's notion that intervention is the cause of the nation's economic ills, prospects for collective action in pursuit of equity and social justice will be drastically diminished.

Since the Reagan victory in 1980 ideological assaults on affirmative government have become increasingly prevalent. Disaffected liberals having lost faith in the outcomes of federal intervention have sought "new ideas" that would reconcile their traditional goals with reductions in the size and scope of government. Implicit in the view of so-called neoliberals is the admission that "old" federal regulatory interventions are no longer applicable to current problems and, given new realities, that little can be learned or gained from prior social welfare initiatives. The neoliberal search for new ideas may yet encourage a healthy reexamination of liberal principles and performance in federal social programs, focusing attention on the appropriate roles of government. Until conservative antigovernment ideology is rejected, however, little progress can be made in extending economic opportunity to all Americans seeking equality under the nation's laws.

REAGAN'S ASSAULT ON OPPORTUNITY

The Reagan administration has paid little attention to the lessons of past federal interventions. Ranging from the attributes of the poor to the record of federal social programs, President Reagan's views of the welfare system run counter to the evidence and experience of recent decades. The economic and social programs of his administration have not reflected a revised approach to problems of poverty and social injustice but rather a complete abandonment of the goal of expanded opportunity in America. President Reagan has ignored sound lessons by advancing a new agenda, one designed to enhance profits and prospects for the affluent while leaving the less fortunate to their own devices.

These reversed priorities are apparent in virtually every aspect of the Reagan record. Making a conscious decision to battle inflation with longer unemployment lines, President Reagan precipitated a deep recession which brought the highest jobless rates since the 1930s and transformed the marginal income losses of rising prices into the total income losses of forced idleness. His sweeping tax and spending reductions further skewed income distribution in favor of the wealthy, slashing federal benefits for low-income Americans while significantly reducing the tax liability of the rich. As a result of these economic and budget policies, an Urban Institute study estimated that average disposable income among the poorest one-fifth of American families will have fallen by nearly 10 percent between 1979 and 1984; during the same period the average disposable income of the nation's wealthiest one-fifth will have remained almost constant.[4]

President Reagan's repeated claims to fairness notwithstanding, his administration has stood the modern welfare system's goal of expanded opportunity on its head by increasing the likelihood of boosting the income of the affluent while diminishing prospects for self-sufficiency among the disadvantaged. During his first year in office Reagan instituted the largest federal tax reduction in history, slashing business taxes by an estimated $169 billion over six years and reducing individual taxes by $500 billion over the same period. The federal income tax cuts were completely offset by increases in federal payroll taxes and the "bracket creep" fueled by inflation for households with annual incomes below $30,000, but families earning $100,000 or more received a tax cut of nearly $9,000 even after payroll tax hikes and inflation. Reagan seldom mentioned that his administration's failure to increase personal exemptions, standard deductions, or the earned income tax credit has significantly raised the total tax liability of low-income families—the average taxes of the poorest one-fifth of American families will have risen by 22.7 percent between 1979 and 1984, and a family of four living at the poverty line in 1982 was required to pay a total of $956 in federal income and payroll taxes.

The Congressional Budget Office has estimated the combined effect of tax and spending reductions under the Reagan administration. Its findings reveal in starker terms the income shift in favor of the wealthy. For households with incomes below $10,000, benefit cuts erased modest tax gains and resulted in a net loss of $130 in 1982, a sacrifice estimated to rise to $240 in 1985. Prospects for households with incomes in excess of $80,000 are dramatically different: they gained a total of $8,320 through the combination of tax and spending reductions in 1982, and their gains are expected to exceed $20,000 in 1985. Middle-income households also received only a fraction of the overall benefits of the Reagan economic program. Households in the $20,000 to $40,000 income range experienced a net gain of $390 in 1982, a paltry sum when compared to the tax savings showered upon the most affluent.[5]

President Reagan has attempted to deflect criticism that his domestic policies are unfair by contending that social spending cuts have been minimal and that they have not affected the safety net protecting the truly needy. If it were not for the refusal of Congress to approve many of Reagan's proposed reductions and for the automatic entitlement to means-tested benefits of those impoverished by the recession, the administration's argument would lose even superficial credibility. With congressional resistance to further spending cuts, however, an expansion of welfare rolls reflecting sharp increases in poverty has offset administration budget savings and pushed total outlays to new heights. In this sense the recession has masked the severity of cuts in individual benefit levels, but a detailed examination of the evidence belies Reagan's claim that he has been fair to the truly needy.

Programs serving low-income Americans have consistently been the object of President Reagan's budget ax, suffering a disproportionate share of proposed spending reductions. Although expenditures for all social welfare programs were trimmed by an average of 7 percent during the first three years of the Reagan administration, those targeted to the disadvantaged have been slashed far more deeply: cutbacks totaled 28 percent in child nutrition programs, 13 percent in welfare and food stamps, 17 percent in compensatory education, and 60 percent in employment and training programs. Spending for means-tested programs dropped from 13.3 percent of total federal expenditures in 1980 to 11.1 percent in 1983, while the share of overall spending devoted to universal programs rose from 40.8 percent to 42.9 percent during that period.[6] An Urban Institute study found that cuts in federal cash and in-kind benefits fell two and one-half times heavier on low-income programs than on others, that more than half of all reductions in state and local grants occurred in programs heavily targeted to poor individuals, and that cuts in social insurance and other programs also hit low-income households hardest.[7] The cumulative impact of this pattern is reflected in the Congressional Budget Office's estimate that the Reagan administration's spending cuts will take more than $20 billion in benefits away from households with annual incomes below $10,000 between 1982 and 1985.[8]

Despite assurances to the contrary the Reagan budget cuts have not spared the truly needy. An estimated 80 percent of reductions in food stamp benefits, totaling $7 billion between 1982 and 1985, have been extracted from families living in poverty. Less than one-tenth of the food stamp cuts enacted by Congress in 1981 and 1982 affected households with incomes in excess of 130 percent of the poverty threshold.⁹ If the Reagan administration's proposed welfare changes had been accepted by Congress, AFDC benefits also would have fallen by more than 40 percent, reducing or eliminating aid for three of every five recipients.¹⁰ In spite of congressional restraint at the federal level, state governments have reacted to the recession and federal budget austerity by reducing average cash welfare benefits an estimated 17 percent. Inflation has further eroded means-tested entitlements for those with no earned income.

The Reagan administration's welfare reductions have fallen most heavily on the working poor. The average real income of 2 million AFDC families with some earnings has dropped by 4 percent and those who barely escaped poverty by raising their income through work suffered the greatest losses. A Congressional Budget Office report on changes in the treatment of earnings in AFDC households estimated that families with earned income would lose 30 to 40 percent of their benefits and 15 to 20 percent of their net incomes, leaving them with little pecuniary incentive to continue working.¹¹ The long-term unemployed also face increasing perils: the number of states that offer AFDC benefits to families headed by a male has dropped from twenty-eight to twenty-one since 1980, and tightened eligibility requirements in the food stamp program have rendered it more difficult for the jobless to qualify for even temporary in-kind assistance.

The Reagan assault on social welfare programs has dramatically accelerated the rise in poverty that started before the Reagan era and diminished opportunities for the least advantaged. Not only did the poverty rate rise from 11.4 to 15 percent between 1978 and 1982 but the average amount of income needed to raise all Americans living in poverty up to the poverty threshold also rose. Adjusted for inflation, the below-poverty threshold deficit of all poor households increased by 11 percent over the 1978–1982 period, rising from $2,370 to $2,630, because wages and cash transfer payments lagged behind the rise in the cost of living.¹² Because federal income transfers accounted for gains against poverty during the preceding two decades, retrenchment in the 1980s has inevitably reversed this progress; not surprisingly, poverty is highest in those states with the most meager levels of cash assistance. Furthermore, reductions in federal support for education, training, job placement, and public sector employment along with the erosion of the statutory minimum wage has hampered the ability of the unemployed and the working poor to achieve self-sufficiency.

Since one-third of all black Americans live in poverty, compared to one-ninth of all whites, the damaging effects of the Reagan program have fallen heavily upon blacks. Households with annual incomes above $20,000 received 80 percent of President Reagan's tax cuts, but proportionately twice as many whites as blacks are members of such households. In contrast, one of every three black households has an annual income of less than $10,000, making them net losers when both tax and spending cuts are considered. The gap between jobless rates for blacks and for whites has widened since Reagan took office, and black teenage unemployment has reached critical levels. Public service employment, a program of federal job creation on which blacks relied heavily for work opportunities, was abolished by the Reagan administration in 1981. Cuts in student and outreach programs for the disadvantaged also darken prospects for blacks in higher education. Finally, President Reagan has sought to narrow the application of civil rights and equal employment statutes and to relax enforcement of these protections, but the Supreme Court has blocked attempts to reverse past progress in opening opportunities for blacks in the private sector.

In retrospect Reagan's safety net certainly was shaped by political expediency rather than any clear concept of social justice or genuine need.[13] The use of safety net imagery to deflect criticism of the Reagan agenda has been confirmed with surprising candor by top administration officials. Former presidential advisor Martin Anderson admitted in late 1983 that "providing a safety net for those who cannot or are not expected to work was not really a social policy objective" of the Reagan administration.[14] David Stockman confirmed that the safety net was a political ploy, referring to presumably protected programs as a "happenstance list, just a spur-of-the-moment thing that the press office wanted to put out."[15] Faced with strong opposition to more equitable budget cuts from powerful special interests, the Reagan administration achieved its overriding priority of reducing the size and scope of government largely at the expense of fairness and compassion for low-income Americans.

Principles of equal sacrifice and protection for the truly needy have survived in administration rhetoric, but they never guided President Reagan's budget ax. Disparities in the administration's treatment of rich and poor have been unjustified and counterproductive, leading Jack Meyer of the American Enterprise Institute to criticize President Reagan's budget reductions for their "unwarranted emphasis on cutting spending for low-income programs coupled with insufficient attention to . . . much larger programs providing benefits to all economic groups."[16] The Reagan program has also violated the American people's sense of fairness in its approach to the truly needy. In an exhaustive study of the administration's proposed reductions in federal social welfare expenditures, University of Utah economist Timothy Smeeding concluded that, had they been fully adopted, "significant decreases in safety net programs for a large majority of the truly needy . . . would have been realized."[17]

The aggregate effects of the Reagan administration's tax and spending cuts will not be apparent for years to come. To the extent that lost opportunities are difficult to quantify, the full impact of today's reductions in child nutrition, education, and training on future generations of wage earners may never be known. Yet it is clear that President Reagan has refused to acknowledge the most basic lesson of the nation's five decades of experience in social welfare policy: that government can make a vast difference by extending opportunities to those who need a helping hand to attain self-sufficiency. By ridiculing federal social welfare efforts and undermining public confidence in government, Reagan has not only halted progress against poverty, but also launched a drive toward selfish individualism which, if allowed to continue, would obliterate the goal of expanded economic opportunity for all Americans.

THE FLIGHT FROM PUBLIC RESPONSIBILITY

Public dissatisfaction with federal social welfare initiatives has grown in recent years, and liberals are partly responsible for the tarnished image of the modern welfare state. The potential for desired change through federal initiatives was frequently oversold, and the unrealistic expectations created by liberal rhetoric contributed to the popular notion that Great Society programs and their successors have failed. Advocates of federal intervention also lost credibility as a result of their reluctance to assess candidly the shortcomings of the emerging welfare system. Established programs developed strong constituencies, thwarting efforts to monitor costs or cap overall expenditures. When combined with public perceptions that federal social programs favored minority groups regardless of merit, the perceived excesses of liberal politics gave credence to charges that federal intervention was ineffective, wasteful, and counterproductive.

The failure of the Carter administration to defend the achievements of the welfare state and contain inflationary pressures in the late 1970s further exacerbated the apprehension and resentment aroused by federal social welfare efforts. Faced with a reluctant and fearful public, President Carter increasingly emphasized efforts to restrain federal spending and reduce budget deficits while attempting to lower public expectations regarding federal responsibilities. As the 1980 election approached there appeared to be little disagreement between Carter and Reagan regarding the importance of battling inflation through restraints on government spending. The choice posed to the American electorate became whether the Democratic incumbent or the Republican challenger could be trusted with implementing this task more effectively.

President Reagan skillfully labeled his 1980 victory a public outcry for less government, claiming a mandate for sweeping reductions in federal responsibilities through a host of budgetary cuts and by repealing regulatory measures. Careful analyses of the 1980 election results provide little support for Reagan's contention that the outcome of the presidential contest represented an affirmation of his assault on government rather than a rejection of Carter's leadership. Although control of inflationary pressures and national security issues dominated the campaign, attitudes toward federal social welfare interventions remained remarkably constant. By margins of three or four to one, Americans continued to believe that the federal government should take an active role in promoting and protecting their economic and social well-being.

The inequities and hardships imposed by the Reagan administration's economic and social policies cannot be construed as merely a response to the demands of an angry public. Reagan's social welfare policies, founded on right-wing ideology, have never been ratified by the voting public, and they deviate sharply from the American commitment to opportunity and compassion which has guided the evolution of the modern welfare system. Following an initial submission to President Reagan's pressures in 1981 Congress has consistently rejected his administration's proposals for significant budget cuts in social welfare programs. The American public believes that some existing federal social programs have been poorly structured and managed, but their call is for greater efficiency rather than retrenchment.

Democrats, following recovery from their 1980 defeat, have increasingly attacked Reagan's misrepresentation of the election mandate and his departure from American values of fairness and compassion. At the same time, however, a new breed of neoliberals has accepted the conservative claim that our economic problems stem from an excess of government. Reacting to the rising inflation of the late 1970s neoliberals have tended to overlook the successes of traditional federal social welfare interventions and proposed new strategies for economic growth that ignore past lessons regarding government's capabilities. By casting federal intervention as a source of the nation's economic problems, neoliberals have also deferred concerns for equity and social justice to another day.

Although fears of broad and rapid economic deterioration resonate with popular wisdom in modern America, it is not clear that the United States has lost either its dominant economic position or its capacity for sustained economic growth and international competitiveness. In a variety of important ways the United States continues to enjoy higher levels of growth and prosperity than either Western Europe or Japan. American living standards are substantially higher than those of our major industrial rivals, and absolute productivity levels also remain the highest in the world—30 percent higher than in Japan and 10 percent higher than in Germany. More strikingly, the U.S. economy generated some 19 million new jobs in the 1970s; Western Europe and Japan experienced no net gain in employment over the same period. These facts do not provide a reason for any less concern regarding poor economic performance since 1973, but they do place in perspective claims that America is on the brink of economic disintegration and technological backwardness.

The American economy's poor performance in recent years can be traced directly to external economic shocks and misguided macroeconomic policies. Rampant inflation and double-digit interest rates during the Carter years were the predictable results of dramatic oil price hikes and heavy reliance on tight monetary policies. Events have been kinder to the Reagan administration, as falling oil and agricultural prices combined with a deep recession have kept inflation at low levels. Yet Reagan's preoccupation with inflation and tax rates has created its own problems—relative price stability has been achieved only through a deep recession and declining national income, while the huge deficits resulting from 1981 tax cuts have placed new pressures on monetary policy and pushed real interest rates to new heights. As an explanation for the troubled condition of key industries and the lackluster performance of the economy as a whole, these shortcomings of macroeconomic policies are far more significant than any burdens imposed by federal interventions to promote social welfare.

In this historical context it is discouraging that neoliberals have focused on "new" ideas to spur economic growth through industrial policies or labor-management cooperation while shunning traditional government interventions. Having acquiesced to the conservative verdict of government failure, neoliberals have no choice but to rely increasingly on cooperation in the private sector to resolve social and economic problems. They offer no evidence to support their hopes for new-found cooperation and consensus in the development of national industrial policies or labor-management relations. Instead, neoliberals have exaggerated both the failures of past initiatives and the potential for less adversarial approaches to economic and social progress.

The debate centering on a new industrial policy provides a useful illustration of the contradictions in neoliberal thought. If industrial policy proposals emerged from another political philosophy, as a vindication of government intervention instead of an alternative to it, their potential for improving economic performance and industrial competitiveness would be considerably greater. With their predominant emphasis on free markets and high technology strategies for economic growth, however, neoliberals have advanced only a cautious and qualified endorsement of government responsibility too weak to counter today's prevailing antigovernment ideology. As a result their analyses have given short shrift to traditional government expenditures for public goods while overestimating the potential for industrial policies that are internally consistent and broadly supported.

Following every economic setback such as the deep 1981–82 recession, calls mount for a planning process that would render national economic policies more explicit and internally consistent. Past efforts have repeatedly failed to build public consensus around explicit policy choices or to avoid divisive political conflicts over competing economic priorities. The 1946 Employment Act and the 1978 Humphrey-Hawkins Full Employment and Balanced Growth Act both attempted to promote macroeconomic policy that would lead to maximizing employment without inflation. The authors of the 1976 National Science and Technology Act similarly sought to ensure that federal priorities in scientific research and technological development were clearly articulated and related to emerging national needs. Successive administrations of both parties, unwilling to risk alienating large segments of the population through explicit policy choices, have ignored these planning mandates in the face of deep political divisions. The wishful appeals of neoliberals for cooperation and consensus are unlikely to alter these fundamental political realities.

Particularly when confronted with the need to allocate federal resources between competing regions and interest groups, politicians demonstrate no enthusiasm for explicit choice. The history of federal regional and local economic development programs certainly suggests that any federal aid channeled directly to industry through industrial policy would be distributed far too widely to correct specific ills. The Area Redevelopment Act of 1961 and the Economic Development Act four years later were enacted in an effort to provide targeted assistance to regions with chronic labor surpluses, but their effectiveness was thwarted when political pressures expanded eligibility from a few dozen labor markets to nearly two-thirds of the more than 3,000 counties in the nation. Targeted aid under the Trade Adjustment Assistance Act suffered a similar fate, pushing program costs to unacceptable levels or diminishing the scope of intervention to the point where lasting change was unattainable. With neoliberals already pledging to help nearly every industrial sector, any new industrial policy would tend to spread the loaves too thinly.

Neoliberal appeals for greater cooperation between labor and management also provide no effective alternative to traditional government interventions. Authoritarian and meritocratic norms are deeply embedded in American culture, and the concept of collaborative decision-making, with its implicit diffusion of responsibility and control, is typically rejected by both management and labor as foreign and counterproductive. The useful principle underlying the concepts of participative management currently in vogue is neither revolutionary nor complex. Any management style that treats workers as individuals with ideas of potential value rather than as cogs in a machine is likely to foster a greater sense of dignity and a more positive attitude toward work. As in the past, insightful managers who base their relationships with workers on mutual respect will nurture interest and good will. Yet the open communication fostered by today's quality of worklife programs cannot obscure the fact that labor and management have distinct and divergent priorities, posing inherent conflicts in the workplace and at the bargaining table.

Concrete solutions to the nation's most pressing economic and social problems will emerge when its political leaders acknowledge—openly, vocally, and unabashedly—the importance of an active role for government. Once illusions of cooperation and consensus are dispelled an effective industrial policy could emphasize public investments to capture the returns associated with an adaptable work force, a strong scientific base, and a sound infrastructure for commerce and trade. Such investments in public goods would build upon a long and proven legacy of government interventions in the economy to educate and train the work force, stimulate research and development efforts, and promote the expansion of trade. However, enlightened policies of this nature will emerge only when the prevailing antigovernment ideology is replaced by a coherent philosophy of government responsibility that acknowledges and proclaims the role of government rather than apologizing for it.

A reaffirmation of basic public responsibilities will not appeal to aspiring politicians touting new ideas, but it will reflect society's continuing attempt to meet age-old challenges: educating the young; feeding, clothing, and sheltering the needy; providing opportunities for the willing. Because free markets fail to secure these prerequisites for opportunity and human dignity, the federal government must intervene to promote the common good. It is regrettable that neoliberals, convinced that the nation's recent past is devoid of progress and useful lessons, are prepared to forsake the powers of collective action through government. Although prior interventions have not always been successful they do provide guidance for resuming the arduous but essential task of expanding economic security and opportunity for all Americans.

THE PURSUIT OF OPPORTUNITY

When the nation's confidence in government is restored the primary challenge of the 1980s will lie in broadening opportunity so that more can share in the nation's affluence. During the past two decades the nation has made substantial progress toward the goal of income security. Federal programs have reduced the hardships of prior boom-and-bust cycles and alleviated the greatest deprivations among the least fortunate. Yet the companion goal of expanded opportunity remains elusive, awaiting a more sustained and adequate commitment of societal resources.

Further progress in social welfare now depends upon restoration of a more acceptable balance between the goals of income adequacy and expanded opportunity in federal policies. The major problems of the modern welfare system—perverse incentives discouraging work by welfare recipients, harsh treatment of the working poor, high youth and minority unemployment, and burgeoning costs of universal entitlements—arise from an inadequate emphasis on the extension of economic opportunity in current policies. Beyond fundamental guarantees of equal access and civil rights, attempts to broaden opportunity have created divisive conflicts between the aspirations of the disadvantaged and the established interests of the more fortunate. Assurances of income security have been easier to adopt, and yet redistributive programs without avenues toward self-support have proved at odds with American values of work and self-reliance. Although a commitment to renewed opportunity will evoke resistance and new uncertainties, no other course can relieve these strains on the welfare system and fulfill the promise of social justice in modern America.

Compensatory Education and Youth Employment

Federal efforts to expand opportunity for future generations must begin with educational programs to establish basic competencies. Without firm grounding in basic skills, the young have little chance to compete in primary labor markets or to achieve self-sufficiency. The employment prospects of youth entering the labor force without the ability to read, comprehend simple instructions, or perform rudimentary mathematical functions are bleak. Many teenagers lacking basic skills have virtually no opportunity to advance beyond unstable, low-paying jobs in secondary labor markets. In order for them to earn a decent wage their low levels of competency must be addressed.

As a long-term strategy prime emphasis should be placed on compensatory education beginning at an early age. Federal funds for this purpose are currently provided under Chapter I of the Elementary and Secondary Education Act, although Reagan administration policies granting local school districts greater discretion in their use may undermine their effectiveness by weakening efforts to target resources on children with the greatest educational needs. President Reagan has also sought unsuccessfully to reduce federal expenditures for compensatory education despite clear evidence that those school districts most in need of remedial services are generally the least able to support them. The appropriate federal role lies in financing mechanisms that seek to equalize educational opportunities across localities and regions and promoting research and dissemination efforts to identify successful approaches to compensatory education.

An immediate strategy for bolstering compensatory education in primary schools should begin with a reinstatement of expenditures safeguards that existed in the Title I program prior to 1981 and a modest expansion of federal appropriations to reach a greater share of the target population through high school. Periodic competency testing, if standardized to preclude serious bias and if coupled with individualized remedial instruction to those who fall behind their peers, can provide a strong foundation for remedial interventions at an early age. This approach is far more constructive than the current response to basic skills deficiencies, adopted in many states, which relies on minimum competency testing as a requirement for high school graduation or its equivalent; it fails, however, to initiate preventive measures at prior stages of schooling. The federal government can play an important role in enhancing the ability to identify and assist children who would otherwise become tomorrow's functional illiterates, providing both financial resources and technical guidance for this crucial effort without interfering with state and local control of public schools.

For today's youth who have already failed in conventional academic settings, federally supported programs should attempt to combine work opportunities with self-paced instruction focusing on basic skills. Past experience suggests that employment alone provides marginal long-term benefits for disadvantaged youth but that structured work experience linked to remedial education can yield more lasting and substantial gains. The most promising strategies for improvement of basic skills emphasize a self-paced approach with clear standards of achievement, thereby accommodating individuals with widely varying competencies and potential. If designed as an integral component of youth employment initiatives, remedial programs can motivate youth previously discouraged by academic challenges and greatly enhance the effectiveness of subsequent job training and placement efforts.

The youth entitlement concept provides a noteworthy response to high teenage unemployment rates and basic skills deficiencies. With school attendance or participation in a high school equivalency program as a prerequisite for obtaining part-time employment, extension of the Carter administration's demonstration projects could lower drop-out rates and increase the effectiveness of in-school remediation efforts. Remedial programs during the school year could lead naturally into the existing summer youth employment program, which should be revised to continue work on basic competencies. Research findings suggest that learning gains achieved during the school year frequently decay over the summer months. Hence, it is essential that in-school remedial programs be closely coordinated with summer youth initiatives to ensure continued academic progress.

The beginnings of an integrated system of compensatory education and youth employment can be found in current federal programs providing aid to poor school districts and job opportunities for disadvantaged youth. Initial extension of a job guarantee to low-income youth in poverty areas could be achieved with a modest expansion of federal youth employment expenditures, assuming limited hours of work and wages at or below the minimum wage. Given appropriate coordination at the federal level, a portion of federal resources channeled to localities through the Job Training Partnership

Act and Chapter I of the Elementary and Secondary Education Act could also be used to develop comprehensive remedial offerings for both in-school youth and high school dropouts. The refinement of program linkages and remediation practices at the local level will occur slowly, and often only through aggressive federal leadership, but the foundation for this essential effort to boost basic competencies is already in place.[18]

An Employment and Training System

The task of broadening opportunity for adults falls primarily upon federal initiatives to promote job training and employment. Since the first formulations of manpower policies in the early 1960s, federal employment and training efforts have been highly decentralized, with wide variations occurring across regions in the level and quality of services provided to the unskilled and disadvantaged.[19] Frequent legislative revisions and administrative shifts have disrupted program continuity at the local level and hampered the development of strong institutional ties between agencies serving the employment and related needs of program participants who face difficulties in holding or competing for jobs.

The policies of the Reagan administration have moved the nation further away from the development of a comprehensive and effective federal employment and training system. Emphasizing private sector placements, low training costs, and local autonomy to the virtual exclusion of other policy concerns, President Reagan has sharply reduced both federal funding for employment and training and federal responsibilities for monitoring the use of such funds under the Job Training Partnership Act. Essential responses to the deficiencies of free markets have also been eliminated: stipends are no longer provided to meet the basic needs of impoverished participants in training programs, and federal job creation programs designed to compensate for the lack of private sector employment opportunities in slack labor markets have been abolished. Driven by ideology rather than prior experience and current needs, the Reagan administration's employment and training initiatives appear certain to provide minimal assistance to the most advantaged among the eligible unemployed while ignoring the pressing needs of the least fortunate.

An effective strategy for expanding opportunity through employment and training programs would differ dramatically from the Reagan administration's approach. Although an emphasis on job placements may give the appearance of cost-effective service, returns on federal investments are maximized when the most disadvantaged are served, when basic skills are increased significantly, and when placement efforts capitalize on this training. Furthermore, evaluations of past initiatives suggest that the quality and sophistication of local training programs vary greatly, necessitating federal efforts to publicize best practices and expand the technical resources available to local program administrators. These federal responsibilities for targeting training stipends and remedial programs to those most in need, as well as for monitoring and improving local service delivery, cannot be abdicated if society's investments in employment and training are to bring maximum returns.

From an individual's perspective, participation in the federal employment and training system should begin with a thorough assessment of personal skills, work experience, and obstacles to employment. For jobseekers with established occupational skills or education credentials, job-search assistance may be sufficient to secure placement in private sector employment. Others with adequate basic skills but no specialized vocational training may be well suited for occupational programs geared to local labor market demands. Finally, those lacking the basic competencies for even entry-level jobs are best served by an intensive program of remedial education, with the successful placed in private or public sector employment or given the opportunity to pursue more specific occupational training. This individualized needs assessment, coupled with varied training and employment options, is the hallmark of a universal system—one that can accommodate needs as diverse as those of minorities, workers displaced by economic change, women suffering the effects of employment discrimination, functional illiterates, and youthful entrants lacking useful skills or work experience.

Regardless of the strength of training and job placement efforts, some portion of the unemployed is always likely to encounter difficulties obtaining work in the private sector. Lack of prior work experience, low skill levels, and discriminatory employment practices all pose barriers to entry for disadvantaged workers, leaving them unable to compete for positions in private business and industry. For these individuals public sector employment serves a dual purpose: it provides adequate income and productive work for persons who would otherwise be forced into idleness, and it establishes a meaningful work record for use in seeking subsequent private sector jobs. Despite the Reagan administration's attempts to denigrate public service employment as wasteful, "make-work" endeavors, federal job creation represents an important investment in the future of the nation's most disadvantaged workers.

Because persons with substantial occupational skills and work experience also suffer prolonged periods of joblessness in slack labor markets, federal job creation efforts should be supported through a two-tier structure. A permanent component should be designed to provide public service employment for those unable to compete in private labor markets. In addition, a countercyclical component should be established to soak up excess unemployment and to stabilize the economy during recessions. Federal expenditures for countercyclical public service employment should be tied directly to an accepted full-employment goal, authorizing funds sufficient to provide jobs for perhaps 25 percent of the total unemployed in excess of a socially acceptable jobless level. Given the countercyclical objective of this second tier, eligibility criteria should place greater emphasis on duration of unemployment and local levels of joblessness than on family income; in most other respects these additional public service employment slots would be identical to those supported through a permanent job creation program.

Wage levels in public service employment must reflect a prudent compromise between frequently conflicting goals. In order not to depress wage rates in local labor markets, incentives to seek private employment are best preserved by limiting total hours of work and earnings while paying participants at existing wage rates commensurate with their skills. For example, secretaries hired by a local government agency might be paid at a prevailing wage rate of $8 per hour, but their hours of work would be restricted to twenty hours per week so that their total earnings do not exceed those available through a full-time job at a minimum wage of $4 per hour. This limit on earnings could be raised for individuals eligible to receive unemployment compensation, giving them a financial incentive to work by allowing them to earn up to 125 percent of their unemployment benefit during their period of eligibility. A pay system along these lines would give temporary public service employees an incentive to seek private sector jobs to increase their total earnings, at the same time acknowledging the market value of their work in the public sector.

The development of a two-tier job creation program will require substantial federal resources. Public service employment is perceived to have failed largely because job creation efforts were mounted too hastily to permit sound administration and too late in each recession to perform a useful countercyclical role. With adequate time devoted to planning and implementation, and with prior authorization of a countercyclical program, the shortcomings of past initiatives can be avoided. The costs of a permanent job creation program to expand opportunity and promote full employment are sizable, but they must be measured against the social and economic costs of inaction. The most recent recession cost the nation an estimated $300 billion in lost income and production, and direct outlays for unemployment compensation totaled $30 billion in a single year. A policy that ignores the losses associated with slack labor markets and forced idleness inevitably will underinvest in the nation's labor force and future economic growth.

Removing Obstacles to Self-Sufficiency

Barriers to advancement can prevent the most motivated individuals from attaining self-sufficiency. Welfare recipients face perhaps the greatest obstacles to upward mobility, confronting marginal tax rates often in excess of 100 percent. The progress of minority groups and women also continues to be impeded by discriminatory hiring and wage practices. They receive lower pay than white males for their occupational skills and educational achievements as well as fewer chances for promotion in primary labor markets. Future gains for all these groups are heavily dependent upon societal investments in education, training, and employment. However, if fundamental incentives to work and assurances of equal opportunity are not preserved, the most enlightened federal interventions in other realms will do little to enhance their eventual self-sufficiency.

The restoration of significant financial work incentives for welfare recipients should be a top priority in federal social policies for the 1980s. At the Reagan administration's behest Congress repealed key provisions of federal income maintenance programs in 1981 designed to encourage recipients to supplement welfare with work and to ensure that work would remain more profitable than dependency. Increasing reliance on in-kind assistance to poor Americans, albeit at reduced levels, has aggravated the problem of work disincentives, leaving some impoverished households subject to the total loss of health insurance or housing assistance when they achieve marginal gains in total earnings. The Reagan administration's unwillingness to allow welfare recipients to retain a reasonable portion of their earned income stands as one of its most egregious assaults on economic opportunity and prospects for advancement.

As an immediate remedy for the high marginal tax rates embodied in current welfare regulations, the Congress should reinstate AFDC provisions that allow recipients to retain part of their earnings without commensurate reductions in benefits. (The law rescinded in 1981 disregarded $30 plus one-third of additional earnings for purposes of calculating welfare eligibility.) Although a more gradual phasing out of federal cash assistance to impoverished households would preclude short-term "savings" heralded by the Reagan administration, it is a prerequisite for renewed progress toward the goal of combining work and welfare in the fight against poverty. Long-term efforts to assist welfare recipients in the transition from dependency to self-sufficiency should also address disincentives associated with federal in-kind aid so that low-income families are not forced to choose between increased earnings and the fulfillment of basic needs. Ultimately, the preservation of meaningful work incentives for welfare recipients requires some sacrifice in the targeting of federal benefits and the containment of overall expenditures. Yet, unless the nation is willing to consign a large segment of the low-income population to permanent dependency, such investments in opportunities for advancement are unavoidable.

In a broader context the federal government has a responsibility to ensure that all members of society have a chance to support themselves and their families through work. In addition to a floor under wages, vigorous enforcement of equal employment opportunity statutes plays a major role in bolstering prospects for self-sufficiency among disadvantaged minorities. The Reagan administration has undermined this foundation for future advancement by defining the concept of civil rights very narrowly and refusing to apply federal sanctions to end discriminatory practices. Past experience clearly indicates that if civil rights protections are reserved solely for cases of proven discriminatory intent, and if remedies are made available only to the immediate victims of such practices, long-standing patterns of employment discrimination cannot be effectively redressed. The Reagan administration's inaction in effect closes the door to economic advancement for disadvantaged minorities.

Federal interventions to broaden opportunity must strike a prudent balance between strengthening the market position of minority workers through education or training and removing obstacles to their progress through legal assurances of equal employment opportunity. While rigid quotas generate strong public resentment and should be reserved for instances of deep intransigence, federal resources should be used aggressively to compensate for the cumulative impact of historic patterns of discrimination and to alter employment practices that are found to have a discriminatory effect. The long-term success of these equal opportunity efforts will be determined in part by the effectiveness of broader initiatives to extend the fruits of future prosperity to the nation's most disadvantaged citizens. Nonetheless, expanded opportunities for women and minorities to enter and advance in the marketplace is a central goal of the modern welfare system.

MENDING THE SAFETY NET

In addition to expanded opportunity the federal social welfare agenda in 1984 should include a reaffirmation of the goal of income adequacy to ensure fulfillment of basic human needs. Given the expanded assistance extended during the 1960s and 1970s to those in need, the present challenge lies primarily in reversing the harsh and counterproductive policies of the Reagan administration which have contributed to a slow unraveling of the social welfare safety net. As federal resources permit, these protections from extreme deprivation should also be refined and strengthened to render them more equitable and compatible with work effort. The extension of limited aid to the working poor should be given highest priority in this regard, justified both as a compassionate response to their needs and a pragmatic means of ensuring that work and welfare go together.

To undo the damage of the Reagan administration welfare policies it will be necessary to halt the vindictive assault on means-tested entitlements and to restore federal budgetary support for programs targeted to low-income Americans. His rhetoric of equal sacrifice notwithstanding, President Reagan has slashed federal expenditures for those in need while shielding the benefits of the more fortunate from significant reductions in federal support. The Reagan administration's "reforms" in AFDC, food stamp, and Medicaid programs, however rationalized, have had the effect of diminishing aid to millions of households with incomes well below the poverty line. Even if Congress had acquiesced to all the drastic cuts proposed by the Reagan administration, these reductions would have helped little in controlling the horrendous federal budget deficits that are the direct legacy of Reaganomics. However, these cuts have weakened the safety net and jeopardized the nation's commitment to help the truly needy.

When aid to the needy is restored to levels that existed prior to the Reagan retrenchments, the absence of a national minimum for federal welfare benefits will emerge as the income support system's most glaring inadequacy. Since the creation of the AFDC program, states have established their own benefit standards for low-income households without a prescribed federal floor to ensure income adequacy. As a result welfare benefits vary widely from state to state, reflecting more the political and economic constraints facing state governments than regional differences in the cost of living. A federal minimum benefit, although perhaps not immediately affordable, should eventually be adopted to promote the equitable treatment of impoverished families residing in less prosperous and generous states. The national conscience should not continue to ignore the wide disparities and low levels of assistance that currently exist.

Extension of federal aid to the working poor is unlikely to be accomplished directly through income transfer programs. Despite the simplicity and efficiency of negative income tax proposals, the demise of guaranteed income schemes during the early 1970s suggests that openly redistributive approaches assisting the working poor will encounter strong political opposition. Adoption of a negative income tax high enough to guarantee basic needs would lead to reductions in work effort sufficiently large to be judged unacceptable by many Americans, and the attempt to preserve work incentives within the negative income tax design would pose sharp conflicts between the adequacy of minimum benefits and the need to contain total program costs. For these reasons enactment of a comprehensive negative income tax program appears politically infeasible in the United States, at least in the foreseeable future.

As an alternative strategy building on existing mechanisms, assistance to the working poor might be most effectively expanded through increases in the federal earned income tax credit and indexing of the minimum wage. The tax credit, which can be refunded in advance to eligible individuals by their employers throughout the tax year, is specifically targeted to workers with earnings below the poverty threshold. It provides a maximum annual credit of $500 for the first $5,000 of earned income, with the amount of the credit gradually decreasing to zero as individual earnings rise to $10,000. The federal minimum wage has stood at $3.35 per hour since 1981, and unless it is tied to changes in average wage levels its significance as a statutory wage floor will steadily diminish.

Although the earned income tax credit fails to offer the comprehensive coverage and equity of negative income tax schemes, its narrower focus on low-income workers greatly enhances its political acceptability, avoiding intractable conflicts with work incentives and work effort among the poor. The further extension of this concept would offer numerous advantages. Serving as an indirect wage subsidy for the working poor, an expanded credit would bolster the real earnings of impoverished households without weakening their ties to the labor market or inflicting the stigma of welfare recipiency. While the Reagan administration championed indexing taxes, it failed to favor adjusting the earned income tax to inflation. Future increases in the earned income tax credit would also help ensure that work remains more profitable than welfare dependency and would not conflict with federal assistance to those who cannot work or are unable to find jobs. Certainly, to the extent that the safety net is strengthened for the dependent poor, the maximum earned income tax credit also should be gradually increased to promote a balanced federal approach to the problem of poverty in America.

Use of the federal income tax system to supplement the meager earnings of the working poor can be effective in meeting most of their basic needs, with one notable exception: adequate health care. Some states currently extend Medicaid eligibility to workers who are "medically needy," but many low-income wage earners still lack health care coverage for either routine doctors' visits or hospitalization. Building on existing programs, a long-term social welfare agenda should include the expansion of Medicaid coverage to the medically needy to all states, so that the working poor and the unemployed qualify for basic health insurance protection on the basis of income. This limited step toward a system of national health insurance necessarily will await progress in mending more recent damage to the nation's safety net. When federal resources permit, the extension of in-kind health care assistance will eliminate an important work disincentive for low-income Americans and reduce their current vulnerability to destitution in the event of serious illness.

In the future, past gains in providing income security and fulfilling basic needs are apt to be most seriously threatened by the continuing rise in single-parent, female-headed house-holds. With the ranks of the poor increasingly filled by women and their dependent children, an effective safety net for the next decade should be supplemented with special assistance for women in poverty. The potential for halting the femin-ization of poverty through federal social welfare policies may be limited—certainly no single initiative could remedy this complex and growing problem. Nonetheless, a foundation for future approaches can be found in two initial steps: federal family-planning efforts should be strengthened in an attempt to slow the growth of impoverished, single-parent house-holds, and child care services should be expanded to remove obstacles to employment and to allow unskilled mothers to participate in federal training and employment programs. Because the restricted work availability and generally low earnings capacity of low-income mothers pose a serious threat of increasing and permanent dependency, the problems of female-headed households in modern America deserve sus-tained attention in the mid-1980s.

AN AFFORDABLE WELFARE SYSTEM

For the social welfare system to remain viable it can be neither deprived of adequate federal support nor overtaxed by nonessential commitments. A comprehensive safety net that reaches previously neglected groups such as the working poor while also addressing the needs of those increasingly exposed to hardship and deprivation can be supported only if the federal tax base is preserved and universal entitlements to the non-needy are curtailed. Defending a sizable tax burden for wealthy Americans in order to broaden the opportunities and fulfill the basic needs of the less fortunate requires strong moral and political commitment, and federal assistance should not be so narrowly targeted that the nonpoor majority perceive no stake in the modern welfare system. The chal-lenge to political leadership lies in clarifying the nation's priorities so that the safety net can be both expanded and trimmed, remaining responsive to the national conscience as well as mindful of the federal purse.

In the wake of the Reagan administration's debilitating tax cuts and huge budget deficits the restoration of the federal tax base is an essential first step toward an affordable welfare state. Sweeping reductions in personal income tax rates for affluent Americans and the virtual abolishment of the corporate income tax have left the federal government bereft of resources and unable to support the most fundamental responsibilities for economic opportunity and social justice as well as national defense. If they are unwilling to abandon the goals of the modern welfare system and to provide for adequate national defense, policymakers have no choice but to reverse President Reagan's irresponsible decision to give away the store to the affluent. Future revisions of the federal tax structure should seek to ensure that wealthy Americans pay their fair share of the nation's tax bill, eliminating the unjustified tax breaks and tax avoidance schemes that now riddle the federal tax base.

Although repeal of the 1981 tax reductions for upper-income taxpayers would go a long way in restoring federal budget solvency, more fundamental tax reforms should be undertaken to promote equity and enhance the future taxable income base. Over the course of the past decade increasing reliance on tax expenditures as instruments of public policy has seriously eroded the federal tax base and undermined the fairness of the progressive income tax structure. Tax shelters have lowered the marginal tax rates for the rich, leaving lower- and middle-income Americans to bear the burdens of increasing federal outlays for defense and domestic programs. Broad public support for the welfare system will be difficult to maintain in the absence of federal tax reforms that more equitably tap all income sources under a progressive tax structure.

The goal of an expanded federal tax base should be applied not only to comprehensive tax reform efforts but also to the curtailment of federal benefits to the non-needy. In an era of massive budget deficits the exclusion of universal entitlements benefits from the taxable income of individuals with other adequate sources of financial support is a luxury the nation can no longer afford. Taxing aid or reducing benefits to nonpoor households—whether through social security, unemployment compensation, or federal pension programs—would enhance the equity of the federal income tax system while reducing the level of social welfare subsidies to those without pressing financial needs. Because few families below the poverty threshold are required to pay federal income tax, substantial savings resulting from this change in the treatment of universal entitlements would conserve scarce federal resources without harming the prospects of the least fortunate.

Equity concerns suggest that recipients of universal entitlement benefits also should not be shielded from the impact of inflation to a greater extent than the average worker. During the 1970s automatic cost-of-living adjustments in most entitlement programs protected the real incomes of beneficiaries even as rapid inflation and stagnating productivity eroded the real wages of working Americans, with total federal outlays soaring as a result. A fairer approach would link benefit levels in federal social programs to increases in average real earnings rather than to changes in the consumer price index. This change was adopted as part of the social security financing compromise in 1983, and it should be extended to other entitlement programs as a constructive cost-saving measure.

The clearest excesses of the modern welfare system can be found in federal assistance to politically powerful interest groups. In some cases, although the goals of federal intervention are appropriate, the means selected to achieve them are inefficient and wasteful. For example, a guarantee of adequate health care for veterans is just and reasonable compensation for their sacrifices in military service. The maintenance of a totally separate and cost-free health care system to treat non-service-connected ailments may, however, be questioned. In other instances, such as agricultural subsidies to corporate farming or lucrative pension benefits for civil service and military retirees, the underlying rationale for federal expenditures itself is subject to challenge. The genesis of these federal programs is evident, and political obstacles to their reform are substantial, but any serious effort to reconcile societal needs and limits to federal resources cannot afford to ignore such obvious departures from sound public policy.

Finally, despite the aversion of conservatives to regulatory interventions, federal planning and regulation occasionally does offer the most effective approach to containing costs in the modern welfare system. The need for regulatory measures is vividly illustrated in the dramatic escalation of federal health care expenditures in recent years. Lacking suitable pricing mechanisms to temper increases in both supply and demand, an equitable health care system that also serves the needy and aged cannot be accommodated within free market models. Congressional reluctance to impose strict controls on medical costs has already precipitated a financial crisis in Medicare, generating fears that the health insurance trust fund will be bankrupt by 1990 and leading policymakers to consider reductions in health care protections for older Americans. Cost-sharing provisions for those who can afford to pay a portion of their own medical bills would alleviate some of the strain on the Medicare system. Nonetheless, a program of health care cost containment that controls rising hospital costs and regulates the construction and utilization of health care facilities offers the only long-term solution that preserves existing social welfare goals.

Beyond selective reductions in benefits to those least in need of federal assistance, the nation's ability to sustain the welfare state depends largely upon a careful weighing of priorities in federal tax and spending policies. The Reagan administration has pursued an ideological program of tax cuts and military expansion to the exclusion of both sound fiscal policy and domestic needs. A more reasoned assessment of acceptable tax burdens and pressing defense needs would permit substantial increases in existing levels of federal support for social welfare efforts. Return to a responsible balance in the eternal "guns-versus-butter" debate is sorely needed.

A COALITION FOR OPPORTUNITY

The task of extending economic opportunities to all Americans is ambitious, but it is not insurmountable. Although finite resources and incomplete knowledge prescribe the absolute limits to our capacity for advancement, the nation's immediate progress hinges more directly on the strength of our resolve. Despite ample evidence that federal efforts to broaden opportunity also promote the common good, recapturing majority support for the modern welfare system looms as a difficult task. Key segments of the traditional coalition for opportunity have undergone wrenching changes during the past decade. Some of society's more fortunate groups have lost faith in the government institutions that have contributed to their affluence, further obstructing a renewed commitment to equity and opportunity.

Hopes for a reawakening of the national conscience ironically stem from the most imminent threats to our past achievements. As a result of its radical departure from American values of fairness and compassion, the Reagan administration has polarized the electorate and reinvigorated political support for the modern welfare system. Confronted with the abandonment of a broad range of federal responsibilities, the voting public has been reminded of the importance of federal interventions to future prosperity. Given forceful political leadership dedicated to equity principles and a vigorous reassertion of traditional federal roles, the potential now exists for reconstructing a majority coalition in support of federal social welfare efforts.

The guiding principles for national progress are to be found less in new ideas than in old lessons and eternal verities. Societal needs—whether food and shelter for the needy, work for the idle, support for the aged, or advancement opportunities for those who have been excluded—have changed little over the decades, and federal interventions have brought significant gains in remedying the deficiencies of free markets. The challenge facing today's political leaders is to undertake a rigorous reappraisal of the modern welfare system, acknowledging its many successes and rebuilding public confidence in government. When this fundamental change in perspective occurs the nation will return to its efforts to fulfill the promise of opportunity in America.

NOTES

1. Ronald Reagan, August 1, 1983.
2. Franklin D. Roosevelt, October 5, 1937.
3. William Greider, "The Education of David Stockman," *Atlantic*, December 1981, reprinted in *Congressional Record* (daily edition), November 10, 1981, p. S13224.
4. Frank Levy and Richard Michel, "The Way We'll be in 1984: Recent Changes in the Level and Distribution of Disposable Income" (Washington, D.C.: The Urban Institute, 1983), p. 3.
5. U.S. Congress, Congressional Budget Office, "Major Legislative Changes in Human Resource Programs Since January 1981," report to House Speaker Thomas P. O'Neill, Jr., August 1983.
    Income Categories," February 1982.
6. Jack A. Meyer, "Budget Cuts in the Reagan Administration: A Question of Fairness" (Washington, D.C.: American Enterprise Institute, 1983), p. 73.
7. Lee Bawden and Frank Levy, "The Economic Well-Being of Families and Individuals," in John L. Palmer and Isabel V. Sawhill, eds., *The Reagan Experiment* (Washington, D.C.: The Urban Institute, 1982), p. 469.
8. U.S. Congress, Congressional Budget Office, "Effects of Tax and Benefit Reductions Enacted in 1981 for Households in Different Income Categories" February 1982.
9. Linda E. Demkovich, "Hunger in America—Is Its Resurgence Real or Is the Evidence Exaggerated?" *National Journal*, October 8, 1983, pp. 2050–51.

10. Timothy Smeeding, "Is the Safety Net Still Intact?" in Lee Bawden, ed., *Reagan's Social Welfare Policy* (Washington, D.C.: The Urban Institute, in press).

11. Linda E. Demkovich, "Reagan's Welfare Cuts Could Force Many Working People Back on the Dole," *National Journal*, January 2, 1982, p. 20.

12. Derived from U.S. Bureau of the Census Annual Current Population Reports, Annual Current Population Reports, Series P-60.

13. James R. Storey, "Income Security," in Palmer and Sawhill, *The Reagan Experiment*, p. 383.

14. Martin Anderson, "The Objectives of the Reagan Administration's Social Welfare Policy," in Bawden, *Reagan's Social Welfare Policy*.

15. Ibid.

16. Jack A. Meyer, "Budget Cuts," p. 120.

17. Timothy Smeeding, "Safety Net," p. 62.

18. Gordon Berlin, *Not Working: Unskilled Youth and Displaced Adults* (New York: The Ford Foundation, August 1983), pp. 42–46.

19. Sar A. Levitan and Garth L. Mangum, "A Quarter Century of Employment & Training Policy: Where Do We go From Here?" (Washington, D.C.: The Center for National Policy, May 1984, in press).

Index

183

ABOUT THE AUTHORS

Sar A. Levitan is research professor of Economics and Director of the Center for Social Policy Studies at George Washington University. He has chaired the National Committee on Employment and Unemployment Statistics and has served on the labor panels of the Federal Mediation and Conciliation Service and the American Arbitration Association. He is the author or co-author of thirty books, including *The Promise of Greatness* and *Human Resources and Labor Markets*.

Clifford M. Johnson is on the staff of the Policy Project in Washington, D.C., and a collaborator, with Professor Levitan, on *Second Thoughts on Work*.